Healthcare Problems and Solutions

GARY FRADIN

HEALTHCARE PROBLEMS AND SOLUTIONS

2008

Healthcare Problems and Solutions

TABLE OF CONTENTS

PREFACE

This book describes healthcare system problems facing America and evaluates three proposed solutions: single payer, managed care and consumer driven. I devote about 2/3 of the book to single payer systems because these currently get the most popular press buzz.

Each solution has positive and negative aspects and each arises from a distinct philosophical orientation and set of social values. I tried to articulate those in respective sections.

I also tried to match overall healthcare solutions with overall systemic problems, for too often proposed solutions focus too narrowly. Some say we have too many uninsured (which we do) and then aim only to expand insurance coverage. Others say that our healthcare is too expensive (which it is) and then aim only to control costs. Still others claim that our care is often inappropriate (which it also is) so aim for more preventive care, more alternative care, or some other direction. Absent a clear definition of the overall systemic problems, discussions about discrete solutions miss their marks.

To this end, I discuss 6 major systemic problems facing US healthcare. This provides a measuring stick and allows us to compare different solutions. These 6 problems are not necessarily definitive or authoritative, though they are commonly accepted as significant. More importantly for our purposes, they are extremely useful analytic tools.

I argue that a healthcare system evolves from a society's values over time. We need to understand both the social values and evolutionary history to decide the applicability of any system for the US.

CHAPTER 1
Orientation

How to look at social system change.

Here's our point-of-departure: the US Institute of Medicine's 2001 report 'Crossing the Quality Chasm' that called for fundamental change to the US healthcare delivery system. The Institute wants a 'sweeping redesign of the entire health system' because 'merely making incremental improvements in current systems of care will not suffice.'

While I agree with the Institute, I generally view actual recommendations for wholesale healthcare system change skeptically. Here's my 3-part lens:

First, beware of utopian social engineering. Karl Popper, the great 20th century British social philosopher warned that utopian social engineers aim to remodel society in accordance with their own plan or blueprint, based on their own values and goals.[1] They arrogantly want to impose their values on others. Utopian social engineers include Karl Marx, Josef Stalin, Mao Tse-tung and Afghanistan's Taliban leaders. They aim to change the entire society and control social evolution. This process creates problems that are huge, avoidable and grave, and always ultimately fails.

The fundamental problem with utopian social engineering according to Popper: the integration of human nature with social change. 'The problems connected with the uncertainty of the human factor force the [planners]... to try to control the human factor by institutional means...*to embrace not only the transformation of society, according to plan, but also the **transformation of man.***' Utopian planners want us to mold men and women to fit into their vision of a new society. This never works successfully.

When healthcare proposals call for eliminating the profit motive from US healthcare, do advocates want to transform only social structures, or also the essential nature of Americans and our society? Some proposals call for healthcare rationing by limiting resources; others for access restrictions. Do these reflect society's values or just the author's? The former may succeed, according to Popper, but the latter will definitely fail.

Second, beware of the impact of bureaucrats and administrators on reform movements. Robert Michels, a famous 20th century sociologist established the Iron Law of Oligarchy [2] which is colloquially: 'Reform movements end when the bureaucrats take over' as administrative processes overwhelm reformists energy. Bureaucratic processes and administrative regulations stifle innovation.

Thomas Jefferson, for example, called for 'a little revolution every so often' precisely to keep administrators from taking over, codifying processes and ending reform movements.

Healthcare administrators and government bureaucrats share an agenda: routinize medical procedures, develop process manuals, standardize healthcare managerial operations and require conformance to established norms. I worry about this because medicine is a young science, too new for overly detailed codification, and still much an art. Medicine has very few processes on which consensus has been achieved and for which detailed data is available; we're still learning and developing. I worry about bureaucrats and administrators acting as gate keepers, imposing process conformance guidelines on medicine and slowing the rate of medical innovation.

Third, note the positive role of competition. Former Nobel Prize winning economist Friedrich Hayek sees competition as a <u>discovery mechanism</u>.[3] Competition according to Hayek, is the process through which people acquire and communicate knowledge. Competition is how society acknowledges that it does not have the information it wants and demonstrates that it is serious about discovering it. Each time we try a new process or service, we learn something about its utility, cost and effectiveness, and use that information the next time. Competition is the best, fastest, most consistent and most reliable long term information feedback mechanism ever developed.

This discovery process relies on experience, not theory. Only true competition can tell us the best way to lower medical prices, how many hospitals we need, which tasks nurses can perform as ably as physicians, etc. As technology advances, demographics evolve and economics change, so do the answers to these and other questions. Knowledge acquisition is an on-going process.

Hayek warns that anything interfering with competition reduces the reliability of information and knowledge gained.

In the real world, of course, society sometimes decides to impose answers—perhaps to promote equity or to protect a public good. Sometimes also special interest groups have enough power to impose their answers. We should understand the trade-offs when this happens; who gains, who loses, what knowledge do we forego and what likely consequences we face.

Popper, Michels and Hayek discuss social evolution from slightly different perspectives—philosophical, sociological and economic—but all arrive at the same general conclusion: incrementalism, based on a society's values, knowledge and understanding, provides a solid basis for social change. Other processes do not. Only incrementalism combines knowledge growth with the evolution of a society's values (a complex interaction and beyond the scope of this book).

We have an underlying tension in this book and in our society. The Institute of Medicine's call for fundamental change stipulates that merely making incremental improvements in our healthcare delivery system will not suffice. But Popper, Michels and Hayek claim that anything other than incrementalism will fail.

Incremental or revolutionary change? Which will work best for us?

CHAPTER 2
Systemic Values

This chapter looks as some social values that a healthcare system expresses.

The US healthcare system is a mess. There is a huge gap between the scientific achievements of American medicine and the delivery failures of the American health care system.[1]

We spend more than any other country on healthcare—some $2 trillion annually—but have 45 million uninsured residents.

We have more medical technology available than any other country—MRI machines, CT scanners and lithotripsy units—but have lower life expectancies than Canada, Costa Rica, Cuba or Chili. [2]

We have brilliant physicians, outstanding technical achievements and world class hospitals—but higher infant mortality rates than Singapore, Sweden, South Korea, Switzerland, Spain or 20 other countries. [3]

How can we explain the gap?

Many believe that the US healthcare delivery system is to blame. That system includes a Byzantine collection of for- and not-for-profit hospitals and insurance carriers, independent physicians, employer-based private health policies, government provided health coverage, Federal healthcare legislation, State healthcare mandates, a myriad of complex tax concerns and a host of related players, incentives and issues.

Each player operates to maximize it's own revenue stream, for absent sufficient cash flow they will cease to exist. No player—carrier, hospital, physician or supplier—operates outside these cash-flow constraints.

Our current fee-for-service based system leads both to expensive healthcare administrative overhead and gross systemic inefficiencies. The net result: less preventive care in America, higher costs and lower life expectancies than other countries.

There is little controversy that we have a healthcare mess. Recent book titles include 'The Healthcare Mess', 'Who Killed Healthcare?', 'Critical Condition', 'Chronic Crisis' and 'Your Money or Your Life'.

Everyone agrees that American healthcare is broken. Unfortunately, not everyone agrees on the solution.

Some believe that we have insufficient governmental regulation and that the appropriate solution to our healthcare problems is more government intervention and regulation. This group often favors a 'single payer' healthcare financing mechanism to solve our healthcare problems.

Others believe that we already have too much governmental interference in the healthcare market, and that the appropriate solution is less government intervention and regulation. In general, this group favors a more consumer driven healthcare financing mechanism.

Still others believe that the appropriate solution lies somewhere in between, but that we need a more 'transparent' healthcare system, with easily accessible data on costs and outcomes. This group may favor a return to true managed care.

How can bright and insightful people look at the same healthcare mess and suggest such vastly different solutions? The short answer: commentators define our healthcare problems differently and make policy recommendations based on different sets of social values.

Some see our high rate of uninsured as the main problem, hold equality of access as a key social value, and proceed from there. Others see cost as the main problem, see continued technological innovation as a key value, and proceed from there. Still others see lack of quality preventive medicine as the main problem and want to promote good healthcare habits as the main goal. And still others want a system that provides everything for everyone though at a lower cost than today.

Based on these different values, there is no one, obviously superior national healthcare system. Canada, Britain, the US Veterans Administration, Kaiser-Permanente and others have developed healthcare systems based on their shared value definitions, however well or loosely defined those values are. These systems evolve as their constituencies evolve.

Thus we cannot establish one, universal yardstick (meter stick?) as an absolute measure of healthcare systemic efficacy. Some societies may prefer economic efficiency (however measured); others equity (however measured); still others extensive personal choices or consumer independence. Some may emphasize prevention, others treatment; some may chose to invest greatly in the elderly or chronically ill while others practice triage, whether by design or default.

The key question is not 'is that healthcare system good from <u>my</u> point of view, based on my values and the units of measure that I think important?' but rather 'does that healthcare system work for that population with its shared historical experience and values?'

Having more MRI machines per capita does not necessarily indicate a better healthcare system; it may indicate an underinvestment in disease prevention. Performing more heart bypass operations per capita may similarly indicate an underinvestment in chronic care or prevention...or it may indicate a superior healthcare system.

Even longevity is not an absolute measure, for investing extensively in octogenarians at the expense of nutrition, childhood education or prevention programs for example, again signifies a social value decision.

As we discuss solutions to our healthcare problems, let's try to understand the underlying values. These are often not well articulated by proponents of one solution or another. And let's try to understand how various solutions will fit with our shared values—however tightly or loosely we share them.

CHAPTER 3
A Statistical Overview

*This brief chapter presents a statistical kaleidoscope of American
healthcare. Readers preferring more description and discussion—and less
data recitation—can proceed directly to the next chapter and use this
information for reference purposes.*

H ere's a snapshot look at American healthcare. We currently
spend about 15% of Gross Domestic Product on healthcare,
compared to [1]

Switzerland and Germany———————	11%
France and Canada———————	10%
Sweden, Holland and Denmark——	9%
Britain———————	8%

Our healthcare expenses have grown since 1950 as a percent of
GDP:

1950———————————————	4% of GDP
1982——————————————-	10%
1990——————————————-	12%
2000——————————————-	14%
2004——————————————-	15%
2014——————————————-	19% [2]

What does this mean for the average American? In 1964, the average
American hourly wage was $2.53, and the average healthcare cost per
individual was $197 annually, so the average person worked about 80
hours (2 weeks) to pay for healthcare.[3]

By 2004, the average American hourly wage rose to $16, and average
healthcare costs per person rose to $6,200 annually, so the average American
worked almost 390 hours (almost 10 weeks) just to pay for healthcare.

Why these huge increases? Since the 1950s our medical technology has improved dramatically. Penicillin and sulfa drugs largely eliminated infectious diseases in the 1950s and 60s. Cardiac catheterization began in 1959. Kidney dialysis, open heart surgery, organ transplants and CT scans were developed in the 1960s and 70s, as were endocrinology, hematology, medical oncology and other specialties. In the 1980s we developed MRI machines, recombinant DNA pharmaceuticals, and materials and techniques for joint replacement. In the 1990s, laproscopic surgeries and additional pharmaceuticals. Medicine is a young science, with the rate of knowledge growth and technological innovation constantly increasing.

Medical technology improvements and expansion of our healthcare sector resulted in American life expectancy (measured from birth) gains of about 7.25 years between 1960 and 2001.[4]

As our healthcare sector expanded and we tracked our medical expenditures, we learned that a very small percentage of our population, and a very small number of diseases, account for most of our healthcare costs. Here is healthcare consumption data: ('consuming' healthcare means healthcare spending on you. If your annual physical costs $400, then we say you have consumed $400 of healthcare, even if your office copayment is only $10.)

1% of our population accounts for 24% of medical costs
5% of our population accounts for 49% of medical costs
10% of our population accounts for 64% of medical costs
50% of our population accounts for 97% of medical costs [5]

So the other (healthiest) 50% of our population accounts for about 3% of medical costs.

In other words, though the 2004 average annual healthcare consumption per American was about $6,200,

The 1% heaviest users (3 million people) averaged about $152,000 each;
The 5% heaviest users (15 million people) averaged about $62,000 each;
The 10% heaviest users (30 million people) averaged about $40,000 each;
The 50% lightest users (150 million people) averaged about $380 each.

About half our healthcare spending goes to 5 diseases: [6]

Mood Disorders
Diabetes
Heart Disease
Hypertension
Asthma

Diabetics, for example, consumed an average $13,232 of healthcare in 2002 compared to non-diabetics' average $2560.[7]

Geriatric spending has also grown tremendously. In 1960, the average American aged 65+ consumed an inflation adjusted $11,495 of healthcare during their remaining lifetime. By 2000, this had grown to an inflation adjusted $147,054. This 11 fold-spending increase directly resulted in life expectancy gains for these elderly Americans of about 1.7 years. [8]

We spend much more than other countries on medical technology. We have more CT scanners (13 per million Americans) than Canada (8) or Britain (6). We have more MRI units (8 per million Americans) than Canada (2) or Britain (4).[9] We perform more coronary angioplasty procedures, more coronary bypass procedures, dialyze more patients, and consume more pharmaceuticals than any other country in the world.

Our decentralized healthcare system reacts more quickly than centralized, single payer systems to technology and treatment changes. This is a mixed blessing. On one hand, American patients are more likely to access the newest technologies available.

On the other hand, this access is extremely expensive, and the lack of coordination among carriers, providers and the government is wasteful. Credible researchers estimate that up to 30% of American medical expenditures are devoted to services that do not provide any detectable benefit.[10] The Institute of Medicine estimates that 14% of bypass surgeries are 'inappropriate.'[11] And the National Committee on Quality Assurance estimates that 57,000 deaths per year are the direct result of failure to deliver 'best-practice care.'[12]

In spite of paying more for healthcare than anyone else, American longevity at birth is lower, and our infant mortality rates higher, than most other developed countries. We're tied for 40th in life expectancy worldwide with Portugal at 77.9 years, behind, among others:

#1	Andorra	83.5 years
#8	Canada	80.7 years
#31	Britain	79.0 years [13]

Our infant mortality rate of 6.9 deaths per 1000 live births doesn't make the top 25 countries worldwide.[14] We exceed

#1	Singapore	3.0
#19	Canada	4.8
#22	Britain	5.0 [15]

Why the discrepancy between high US healthcare costs and low US healthcare outcomes? We'll turn to some underlying reasons in the next chapter.

CHAPTER 4
Six Healthcare System Problems

This chapter outlines 6 systemic problems that currently plague US healthcare: (1) the Uninsured, (2) the Medical Arms Race, (3) Moral Hazard, (4) Ineffective Chronic and Preventive Care, (5) Uneven Quality and (6) Low Quality and Safety.

Milton Friedman, the Nobel Prize winning economist, looks at the information presented in the last chapter with wonder. Why is it, he asks, that in every other field where enormous technological strides have been made, total costs have fallen over time, but in healthcare they have increased? 'In every other part of the economy, growth in an area has been accompanied by declining unit costs and declining percentage of national income,' he says.[1] But not in healthcare.

I propose answering his question by identifying and discussing 6 major systemic problems that currently plague American healthcare: [2]

(1) The high number of uninsured Americans;
(2) The medical arms race;
(3) Moral hazard;
(4) Ineffective chronic disease care and prevention;
(5) Uneven treatment quality nationwide, and
(6) Relatively low quality and safety investments.

Once we understand these underlying problems, we can evaluate various healthcare improvement options to see how they address these issues.

Problem #1: The 45 million uninsured Americans. The Institute of Medicine noted that working age Americans without health insurance are more likely to:

- Receive too little medical care and receive it too late;
- Be sicker and die sooner;
- Receive poorer care when they are hospitalized.[3]

The uninsured often go without appropriate care. For example, they more often

- Go without cancer screening tests thus delaying diagnoses;
- Do not receive care recommended for chronic diseases, like timely eye and foot exams to prevent blindness and amputations in people with diabetes;
- Lack regular access to medications to managed conditions such as hypertension;
- Receive fewer diagnostic and treatment services after a traumatic injury or heart attack.

The IOM summarizes its findings as

'The health and length of life of working-age Americans would improve if they obtained coverage…they would use preventive services more often and would be less likely to delay seeking care, thus making early detection and treatment of problems more feasible.'

The US stands alone among industrialized nations with millions lacking health coverage. This is clearly a major healthcare systemic failure.

Problem #2: The Medical Arms Race. The Medical Arms Race describes competition among hospitals for physician referrals and patients. Hospitals compete with each other by offering the latest in medical technologies and most modern facilities, often at great expense and sometimes without indications that the newest technologies significantly improve outcomes.

Why is this? Physicians want to refer to the most up-to-date facility, patients want treatment at the same, and malpractice lawsuits may be lost for failure to use the latest and best technologies. No one wants to use a hospital with old machines or old technologies—even if these work perfectly well. When a new machine or technology becomes available, all hospitals in a competitive environment purchase it—for fear that if they don't and their competitors do, their referral sources will dry up and they'll go out of business.

Our fee-for-service or cost-plus insurance reimbursement formulas encourage this proliferation of costly medical technologies. Under fee-for-service, as a hospital's costs increase, so do it's fees. Under cost-plus reimbursement, the 'plus' calculation is generally a fixed percentage of 'cost'. So as a hospital's costs increase, so does its 'plus' reimbursement— and it makes more money.

The medical arms race was perhaps initially identified in 1985 when economists James Robinson and Harold Luft discovered that hospitals with <u>more</u> competitors had <u>higher</u> costs of care, staffing levels and high tech medical equipment than hospitals without competitors, because they had to keep up with their competitors.[4] Counterintuitively, they also found that these competitive hospitals often had poorer treatment outcomes than non-competitive. Here's why:

> Medical researchers have known for years about the volume-outcome relationship in medicine. Hospitals, surgical teams and surgeons with the most experience in specific procedures have the lowest mortality rates, and those with the least experience have the highest mortality rates. This stands to reason as 'practice makes perfect'. By spreading the same number of procedures over more hospitals and surgical teams, the medical arms race may reduce the amount of experience of each team—leading potentially to higher mortality rates.[5]

Here's a case study from Indianapolis that illustrates these points. In 2002, insurance reimbursements for coronary by-pass surgery in Indianapolis generated an average hospital bottom line of about 23%— quite good for any business.[6] To take advantage of these margins the Heart Center of Indiana opened a new 60 bed cardiac unit. This triggered their medical arms race. Between 2002—2004, Indianapolis' 4 other major hospitals invested $220 million to renovate, expand and add 20% new cardiac capacity, making a total of 5 cardiac centers for 1.6 million people.

Unfortunately, there was no evidence of need: open-heart volumes had been falling for 2 years from 4,377 procedures in 2002 to 3,310 in 2004. Not to worry suggested Tom Malasto, Executive Director of the Cardiac and Vascular Care Center at St. Francis Hospital in 2004. 'The most recent CDC statistics place Indiana as one of the top five states for obesity and prevalence of smoking'.

The Indianapolis facilities chose to wait for—or induce—demand for expensive heart surgeries. Rather than invest in obesity prevention, low cost treatments or smoking secession programs, huge investments went into expensive surgical facilities. Had this been normal economic competition, we would expect the various producers to segment their market—one supplier aiming at expensive procedures, another at low-cost alternatives, still another focusing on prevention—and then advertising for customers. Or, if all suppliers aimed at the expensive market segment, we would expect prices to fall.

But prices don't fall when hospitals compete. No surgeon wants to operate in an older (read: second-rate) facility, and no patient wants second-rate care. Once the Heart Center of Indiana opened it's new 60-bed facility in 2002 all the other hospitals had to follow. They needed to keep their cardiac surgeons happy or feared losing them to the new Heart Center. Jack Finn, director of the New Orleans Metropolitan Hospital Council explained why 'When you get hospital competition in a city it drives costs up, not down. The competition is for doctors, not patients. And if you're going to compete for doctors, you have to have state-of-the-art equipment.'

But by spreading a decreasing number of coronary procedures over more hospitals and surgical teams, mortality risks may increase. Indeed the Leapfrog Group, a respected medical industry think-tank that monitors hospital quality and safety recommends a 450 coronary bypass surgery annual hospital minimum; below that, the mortality rates increase.

If the number of heart surgeries in Indianapolis continues to decline to as it had from 2002—2004, then by 2007 or 2008 all 5 cardiac facilities will average fewer than 450 by-pass surgeries annually—below the recommended safety volume. This appears the case: according to the Leapfrog Group website (leapfroggroup.org) in December 2007, Indianapolis' St. Vincent Hospital annually performs just 344 coronary artery bypass procedures annually—only 76% of the recommended safety minimum.

(Interestingly, Leapfrog also recommends a minimum 120 aortic valve replacement procedures annually. St. Vincent's only performs 30. St. Vincent's did, however, score higher for some other high-risk coronary procedures.)

The Medical Arms Race forces American providers invest huge amounts of money in (unnecessary?) technologies and possibly increase mortality risks for patients, while ignoring alternative treatment options.

There is a second version, at least, of the Medical Arms Race. Hospitals invest in, for example, expensive new high tech screening tests designed to spot cancers early, far more than they invest in nutrition and exercise programs (see below 'Ineffective Chronic Disease Care'). Carriers reimburse well for these tests and investments; hospitals keep their referrals coming and—theoretically—patients benefit.

Here's the dual problem. **First**, the cost/diagnosis is high—and the cost per <u>marginal</u> lifesaving diagnosis extremely high. (A marginal lifesaving diagnosis is the problem that an existing technology would miss with negative patient outcomes, but a new technology finds with positive outcomes. Often the existing technologies would pick up the problem in time for treatment.)

Second, the new, expensive new technologies lead to many false positives—results that indicate patients might have cancer when, in fact, they do not. Patients consequently undergo stressful, expensive follow-up tests and procedures. The Boston Globe reports that doctors perform an estimated 2 million biopsies annually on <u>healthy</u> breasts in women and prostate glands in men as a result. The Globe also reports that more than 500 women with no symptoms of ovarian cancer underwent unnecessary abdominal surgery because tests wrongly suggested they had the disease.

'There is a vast ocean of potentially diagnosed, but clinically meaningless cancers' according to Dr. James Talcott, director of the center for outcomes research at the cancer center at Massachusetts General Hospital. 'The more you [test] the more of those meaningless cancers you're going to find.'[7]

In this version of the Medical Arms Race, we invest huge sums to gain a marginal diagnostic advantage, then more money to explore the false positives. Hospitals all compete to offer these 'newest, greatest' tests and keep their physician network referring.

The tragedy: we could save more lives and improve more people's quality of life by investing in prevention and chronic disease treatment for the masses. But that's not how hospitals compete.

<u>**Problem #3: Moral Hazard.**</u> 'Moral hazard' identifies how behavior changes when an insurance company pays: we have more doctor visits, tests and procedures than if we paid individually, out-of-pocket. We shop less wisely or aggressively using the insurance carriers' money than our own.

The moral hazard concept originated in the fire insurance industry when executives became concerned that people with 'poor moral character' might purchase policies and then burn down their own houses to collect the insurance proceeds. Flood insurance companies worried that people with flood insurance might build in flood plains—figuring that the insurance company would pay to rebuild should a flood occur. Auto insurance carriers concern themselves with policyholders who intentionally cause auto accidents to gain insurance benefits. And health carriers worry that people will have expensive, unnecessary medical tests and procedures.

Healthcare moral hazard is an elusive, difficult to grasp concept. Much like former US Supreme Court Justice Potter Stewart's description of pornography, it's hard to define but recognizable upon sight. Moral hazard is healthcare systemic inefficiency. We'll use three definitions.

First, healthcare efficiency means 'having the patient get all care that is worth at least what it costs, but get no care that is worth less than what it costs'. Moral hazard is the opposite: patients may get care worth less (in terms of longevity gains or life quality improvements however measured) than the costs.

Second, healthcare efficiency might be 'the treatment plan that your physician who is well versed in the current medical literature and knows your medical condition well, would approve absent any economic considerations.' Moral hazard is the opposite—a treatment plan that includes economic considerations. A patient might say 'I don't know if I really need this test or procedure, but it's free (to me) so I might as well have it.' A provider might say 'I don't know if the patient really needs this test or procedure, but it's free (to them) and I can bill the insurance carrier, so I might as well do it.'

Third, healthcare efficiency means 'getting the maximum treatment benefit at the lowest cost.' When moral hazard enters the picture providers might recommend beneficial but costly treatments and ignore equally (or more) beneficial but less expensive remedies.

Under most US health insurance payment programs, providers receive fee-for-service payments, often calculated as cost-plus reimbursement. Physicians only get paid if they perform a service. Hospitals get paid only if they treat. The physician or hospital has a financial interest to treat and earns the most by providing the most expensive treatment. Meanwhile the patient has little or no financial interest in receiving low cost treatment or avoiding treatment altogether.

Economist Milton Roemer initially quantified this phenomenon in 1961.[8] Roemer studied hospital admission behavior in an upstate New York community and developed Roemer's Law: that a hospital bed built is a hospital bed filled. In 1957 this community had 1 general hospital with 139 beds that seemed to meet community needs with an average daily census of 108—suggesting that the hospital was rarely full. In 1958, the hospital moved to a new facility with 197 beds and the occupancy average increased to 137 (a 26% increase in 1 year)—with no change in the overall community health and no other economic factors at work.

Roemer's only explanation: physicians responded to the increased supply of beds by admitting more patients. He finds that 'the supply of hospital beds in a community or state is the major determinant of the hospital utilization rate.' Physicians and hospitals are paid fee-for-service by insurance companies; they only get paid when they treat, thus creating an economic inducement to over-treat or over-hospitalize.

Dartmouth Medical School researchers have followed Roemer's lead and extensively studied economic effects of moral hazard in fee-for-service medicine. Dr. Elliott Fisher, a highly respected Dartmouth researcher, summarizes the impact of moral hazard on US healthcare: 'up to about a third of medical care is devoted to services that do not provide any detectable benefit.' [9] This is close to Roemer's discovery of a 26% increase in (unnecessary?) hospitalizations. Dr. Fisher also notes that increased levels of medical treatment sometimes lead to worse results (due to infections, physician errors, lack of attention to prevention, etc).

Here's a quick case study.[10] In 2001 Medicare paid for 6.9 back surgeries per 1000 enrollees in Fort Myers, Florida. But it only paid for 3.2 back surgeries per 1000 enrollees in Miami. The national average was about 4.5. Had Fort Myers operated at Miami's rate from 1992—2001, Medicare would have saved almost $2 billion: 4,800 surgeries at an average $40,000 each.

Why the discrepancy in back surgery rates for the same epidemiological population? 'It's highly improbable that Medicare retirees living in Fort Myers prefer back surgery two times as often as residents of Miami' suggests James Weinstein, Chairman of Dartmouth Medical School's Department of Orthopedic Surgery. Rather, he looks at the 'surgical signature' of doctors—- idiosyncratic patterns in the likelihood of a doctor choosing to operate. The greater the scientific uncertainty in treatment options, he suggests, the more variations appear.

GARY FRADIN

And the more opportunity for moral hazard mischief. In 2001, according to a study done by the American Academy of Orthopedic Surgeons, spine surgery accounted for more than half of all profits from orthopedic procedures in hospitals, but only 21% of the volume. Spine surgeries can be very profitable.

Surgeons at 3 hospitals owned by Lee Memorial Health System, a 'leading provider of healthcare in Southwest Florida' according to their website, performed 447 spine procedures on Medicare patients in 2004. Medicare reimbursements to the 3 hospitals for spine operations grew by nearly 50% in the previous 5 years.

'I can't explain it' says Chuck Krivenko, Lee Memorial's chief medical officer when shown the back surgery rate statistics. He suggested that surgery is about the best medical intervention available for back pain. But he noted that 'if the only tool you have is a hammer, everything looks like a nail.' Carrier reimbursement practices and hospital profitability goals, of course, may influence the perception that 'everything looks like a nail'.

Dartmouth's Weinstein disagrees. Dartmouth-Hitchcock Medical Center provides patients with education and options. 'What we have found is that patients tend to make good decisions when presented with good information.'

As a result, in 2001 Dartmouth-Hitchcock, working with the same Medicare epidemiological population as Lee Memorial, performed back surgery on 2.3 Medicare patients per 1000 beneficiaries—1/3 as much as Lee Memorial, and even less than Miami!

Why does our healthcare system allow all this waste? Commentators suggest that providers, carriers and consumers have separate sets of interests.

Providers get paid to treat, so have their financial interests tied to providing as much treatment as justified, not as little. Sick patients typically present with multiple problems (e.g. high blood pressure, coronary issues and pulmonary issues simultaneously) and thus complex diagnoses. The responsible, reasonable and thorough physician examines all problems and evaluates all potential medical issues while diagnosing, and presents all potential treatment plans when treating. Are all diagnoses and treatments equally necessary? Unclear. If the patient paid out-of-pocket, would the physician and hospital services be more limited? Also unclear. But Dartmouth's Dr. Fisher seems to suggest, likely.

Patients want as much treatment as possible. After all, they fear that their medical problem may be significant and they have insurance to cover medical expenses. Many studies have found that patients use medical services as long as the probable benefits outweigh their co-payment cost (often $10-20). This is classic moral hazard: the patient only pays a small percentage of treatment costs, so faces an artificial cost-benefit analysis.

Patients also have significant difficulty determining which physicians and hospitals provide the highest quality service as our medical system provides notoriously poor outcome data. Absent this information, consumers take 2 opposing directions when purchasing health insurance and healthcare:

> **First**, they substitute physician trust and credentials for knowledge of physician quality. They trust, for example, a kind and responsive PCP as they cannot determine whether or not he/she is really 'good'. They trust doctors at Massachusetts General Hospital (or the Cleveland Clinic, or the Mayo Clinic, or other) more than a local community hospital because 'Mass General is world class, many physicians went to Harvard and it's simply—obviously—better than the others' with no data to back up these claims. Mass General is more expensive than most other Boston area hospitals. But consumers don't care because they don't pay;

> **Second**, these consumers also demand wide provider choice and few referral restrictions when choosing health insurance. This allows them to change providers should they so desire. 'It is a sad irony that 'choice of doctor' has become in most American's minds, the single greatest measure of the quality of any health care plan,' claims Phillip Longman, author of <u>Best Care Anywhere</u>.[11] Consumers demand this choice because they lack information about provider quality and treatment outcomes.

Carriers want to satisfy their customers. As consumers demand easier referrals and wider provider networks, the carriers comply. HMOs—with referral restrictions that help reduce moral hazard waste—have lost market share to PPO/POS plans with few if any referral requirements, according to the Kaiser Family Foundation: [12]

Plan Type	Percent of US Health Insurance Policies by Year		
	1996	2000	2005
HMO	31%	29%	21%
PPO/POS Combined	42%	63%	76%

And many HMO referral restrictions have diminished over time.

As these three parties—providers, consumers and carriers—all pursue their separate interests, moral hazard waste grows and our healthcare inflation roars...but healthcare results don't necessarily improve.

Problem #4: Ineffective chronic disease and preventive care.
Medical conditions can usefully be divided into two types: 'chronic' and 'episodic.'

Chronic medical conditions are long-term, often presenting multiple, inter-related medical problems. Diabetes is such a chronic condition, often caused by obesity and requiring a coordinated team of specialists and technicians, including endocrinologists, psychologists, podiatrists, nephrologists, nutritionists, educators and others for proper treatment. The chronic condition is never 'cured'—the disease is only 'controlled', requiring an on-going, long-term effort.

Episodic conditions are one-off. Once treated and rehabilitated, the patient returns to good health without much need for on-going medical treatments. Episodic conditions and treatments include broken bones, illnesses such as pneumonia, and many coronary procedures.

The US fee-for-service provider payment system is primarily episodically based, with providers billing by Diagnostic Related Group (DRG) or a similar accounting system. Medicare initially developed DRGs in the 1970s as a cost-control mechanism. The Institute of Medicine claims in Crossing the Quality Chasm that 'today's health system remains overly devoted to dealing with acute, episodic care needs.'

The Top 10 DRGs by Case Volume in 2002 were [13]

DRG Number	DRG Description
127	Heart Failure & Shock
089	Simple Pneumonia & Pleurisy
088	Chronic Obstructive Pulmonary Disease
209	Major Joint & Limb Reattachment
014	Intracranial Hemorrhage & Stroke
296	Nutritional & Misc Metabolic Disorders
182	Esophagitis, Gastroent & Misc Digestive Disorders
174	G.I. Hemorrhage
143	Chest Pain
138	Arrhythmia & Conduction Disorders

Yet the majority of US medical problems are chronic disease-based. Chronic disease treatment requires multiple healthcare interactions every year to ensure small but steady advances that can prolong life. Ranch Kimball, President of Boston's Joslin Diabetes Center laments that

> While [Massachusetts'] healthcare system is the best worldwide in helping acutely sick people, it is poorly organized to prevent chronic disease or to intervene early enough to prevent complications.[14]

More than half of all Americans have at least one chronic illness, Kimball reports. The American Diabetes Association estimates the direct medical costs of diabetes in 2002 alone were over $95 billion, more than double the 1997 bill.

Thirty years ago—in the era when DRGs were developed—patients presented primarily with specific episodic medical issues such as heart attacks. Today however, perhaps 75% of our healthcare costs go to treating patients with chronic conditions, often a combination of obesity, hypertension, diabetes and depression. (One potential reason: our episodic treatments are so successful that people live through the medical episode and have a chance to develop chronic conditions.) Indeed, Emory University's Professor Kenneth Thorpe suggests that obesity related (i.e. chronic) conditions alone may account for up to 1/3 of the total US healthcare cost increases over the past 15 years. [15]

What happens when chronically ill patients meet an episodically based hospital reimbursement system? Here's a case study of Manhattan's Beth Israel Medical Center's diabetes center.[16]

In March, 1999, Beth Israel opened its diabetes center, designed as a 'boot camps for diabetics...The center would teach them to check [blood sugar] levels, count calories and exercise with discipline, while undergoing prolonged monitoring by teams of specialists.' In other words, a moderately long-term, team approach to a chronic disease.

One patient, Ella Hammond a retired school administrator, compared Beth Israel to other preventive care. 'The center was a totally different experience. What they did worked because they taught me how to deal with the disease, and then they forced me to do it' in twice weekly, two-hour classes…compared to the average physician office visit lasting about 8 minutes. Hammond attributed her 20-pound weight loss to those classes. 'I needed reminding.'

The program was 'an unqualified success' according to the New York Times. Within 5 months more than 60% of the center's patients had their blood sugar under control. Close to half had lost weight. Competing hospitals directed their diabetic patients to Beth Israel. Patient volumes grew by 20% monthly as success stories spread.

But Beth Israel lost money—$1.1 million. And within 10 month the hospital decided to close its diabetes program. Why?

Carriers pay more for sickness procedures than wellness visits. There is no DRG for 'reducing a patient's blood sugar level'. Insurers often balk at paying $75 for diabetic's regular nutrition counseling, but regularly pay $315 per kidney dialysis session—a byproduct of diabetes.

Insurers also often refuse to pay $150 for a diabetic's regular preventive podiatric visits, but will pay $30,000 for a foot amputation, apparently thinking that they will save $150 this year and that you'll switch to another carrier before you need the amputation.

And carriers paid only $25 for an hour-long diabetes class. 'That wasn't even enough to pay for what it cost to have me do the paperwork to get the reimbursement' according to Denise Rivera, the Center's secretary.

The Beth Israel program scheduled patients for multiple physician and educator visits per day—for patient convenience and education reinforcement. But Medicaid only pays for 1 service per person per day. So every time the hospital scheduled a diabetes education class and a specialist visit on the same day—in other words, worked in the patient's best interests—it lost money.

Beth Israel learned the lesson that insurance carriers already knew. 'The point is not to attract the most customers but rather the best… insurance executives usually think twice before bolstering their diabetes benefits, for fear they will attract the chronically ill,' according to the New York Times article on Beth Israel's program.

The result: Beth Israel closed its successful diabetes treatment program precisely because it was successful. More diabetics went untreated, suffered (preventable) blindness, limb loss, kidney failure or other problems, and the ultimate, episodic treatment costs continue to soar.

Interestingly, Boston's Joslin Diabetes Center has taken an alternate financial approach. Roughly 40% of Joslin's diabetes care is not reimbursed by insurance. Joslin realizes that our episodic-based health insurance reimbursement formula fails patients (apparently about 40% of this time), so arranges outside, non-insurance funding to continue it's patient based diabetes treatments.

What is the economic impact of our current ineffective chronic disease management? The Milken Institute (October 2007) estimated the economic and business costs of the 7 most common chronic diseases—cancer, diabetes, hypertension, stroke, heart disease, pulmonary conditions and mental disorders—at $1.1 trillion annually, due primarily to lost productivity. The Institute also reports that over 109 million Americans have at least one of these 7 diseases, with incidence rising. Better obesity prevention and treatment alone could generate productivity gains of $254 billion annually and avoid $60 billion in treatment expenditures per year...not to mention, alleviate untold suffering by the patients and their families.

There is a second aspect of poor preventive care—the inefficacy of annual physicals. Some 64 million Americans get their physical annually at a cost of almost $8 billion.[17] But researchers question the scientific justification of this. No major clinical organization in North America supports annual physicals as a standard. Listening to heart and lungs probably doesn't help unless the patient has symptoms; same for a complete annual blood count, urinalysis, EKG and X-ray.

The annual physical ritual, as currently practiced, has three drawbacks. **First**, they waste expensive physician resources. 'If I'm spending 20 minutes or half and hour with you on an exam that's not necessary, that's 20 minutes I could be spending with one or two other patients who are ill,' say's Dr. Robert Goldsizer, associate chief medical officer at Boston's Brigham and Women's Hospital. 'That's waste.'

Second, the 20 minute overview is insufficient for the physician to understand underlying patient issues and provide advice and support. The patient may suffer from physical or emotional stresses that Marcus Welby-type physicians could address. Indeed, the annual physical is theoretically the time for patients and doctors to talk, develop trust and explore medical issues. But 20 minutes is too short. Patients may need more time to open-up and divulge potentially embarrassing but important information; physicians may need more time to pursue discussions. The downside: a patient gets a good bill of health and feels praised by the physician—based on unnecessary tests—while the underlying issues remain untreated.

Note that the 20 minute time frame results from insurance carrier pressures that physicians see more patients per time period, rather then generate better results per patient. This runs exactly counter to the Institute of Medicine's 'Crossing the Quality Chasm' recommendations that defined medical care as a relationship, not just a visit. Donald Berwick, President of the Institute for Healthcare Improvement, claims 'the main population need today is for continuing relationships over time and place, integrating care with a memory'[18]—not quickie, impersonal visits.

Third, the annual physical functions more as early disease <u>detection</u> than disease <u>prevention</u>. We know, for example, that regular exercise prevents far more diseases than an annual complete blood count. Yet at your physical, your caring physician only has time to say 'exercise more'—without detailing a specific program or designing an effective follow-up procedure.

Harvard Magazine presents this case compellingly, describing a wonder-pill:

> In the bottle before you is a pill, a marvel of modern medicine that will regulate gene transcription throughout your body, helping prevent heart disease, stroke, diabetes, obesity and 12 kinds of cancer—plus gallstones and diverticulitis. Expect the pill to improve your strength and balance as well as your blood lipid profile. Your bones will become stronger. You'll grow new capillaries in your heart, your skeletal muscles and your brain, improving blood flow and the delivery of oxygen and nutrients. Your attention span will increase. If you have arthritis, your symptoms will improve…You will test younger according to a variety of physiologic measures. Your blood volume will increase and you'll burn fats better. Even your immune system will be stimulated…[19]

The only problem—there is no such pill. The prescription is exercise. But your harried physician in your 20 minute physical can only prescribe an actual pill that accomplishes some of this—not manage an exercise program to address all of it. Remember the experience of Ella Hammond, the retired school administrator working with Manhattan's Best Israel diabetes program. Reinforcement, repetition and support worked; a one time admonition with Rx does not.

The underlying problem: physicians get paid to intervene, not to prevent. There is no DRG for listening to patients or probing into their emotional/physical issues. There is no billing code for providing excellent preventive care. Physicians do not get paid to monitor your exercise regime; they get paid to treat you after you and they fail to prevent illnesses.

Problem #5: Uneven treatment quality. Researchers have known about regional medical treatment variation for years. An early study 'Are Hospital Services Rationed in New Haven or Over-Utilized in Boston' [20] reported that rates of certain procedures including coronary artery bypass graft surgery were much higher in New Haven than Boston, but that rates of other procedures such as carotid endarterectomy here higher in Boston than New Haven.

Another study showed that 20% of the children in Waterbury Vermont had their tonsils removed by age 15, but in next-door Stowe, 70% did.[21] These differences could not be explained by socio-economic differences or by differences in, for example, the town water.

Researchers, led by John Wennberg, Elliot Fisher and others at Dartmouth Medical School discovered other significant regional treatment variations. Medicare spends, for example, twice as much on enrollees in Miami as on enrollees in Minneapolis with the same age, socio-economic and health status.[22] The same holds for Medicare beneficiaries in Manhattan ($10,000 in 2003) vs. beneficiaries in Portland, Oregon ($5,000). [23]

They also learned, oddly enough, that the more expensive hospitals often provided the worst treatments. Heart attack patients in high spending hospitals, for example, only receive aspirin 75% of the time upon discharge, whereas patients in low spending hospitals do 84% of the time. And patients in high spending hospitals get fewer flu vaccines (48% to 60%) than do patients in low spending.[24] Even though residents of high spending areas received more care, they did not

'have lower mortality rates, better functional status or higher satisfaction...these differences in spending were explained almost entirely by greater frequency of physician visits, more frequent use of specialist consultations, more frequent tests and minor procedures, and greater use of the hospital and intensive care units'[25]

These treatment variations indicate systemic quality problems. Failure to practice evidence-based medicine and follow 'best practice' guidelines costs both money and lives.[26] One structural reason for these quality problems: the notorious failure of US medicine to quantify and publish outcome data—five year mortality rates from bypass surgeries, hospital infection rates, etc.

Problem #6: Relatively low quality and safety investments. The Institute of Medicine defines quality as 'the degree to which health services for individuals and groups increase the likelihood of desired health outcomes'[27] and bluntly states 'The U.S. healthcare delivery system does not provide consistent, high-quality medical care to all people.'[28]

In 1999, the Institute issued 'To Err in Human' indicating that up to 98,000 people die of medical or medical systemic errors annually. These errors include diagnostic, treatment, preventive and systemic problems. The IOM believes that faulty systems, processes and conditions, rather than individual physician mistakes are the root causes. [29]

The Centers for Disease Control and Prevention estimate that hospital acquired infections—almost entirely preventable—account for another 90,000 deaths annually.[30] And the RAND Corporation estimates that another 126,000 die due to their physician's failure to observe evidence-based medicine for 4 common conditions: hypertension, heart attack, pneumonia and colorectal cancer. [31]

What are some specific system ills? First, the US has no national database of citizen health. Your primary care physician has some information; the hospital that performed your colonoscopy has other, your specialists have still others. Should you suddenly become ill, physicians likely will be unable to review your medical past—putting them at a diagnostic disadvantage and you at unnecessary risk.

Second, many American providers have notoriously inefficient, non-networked, information technology systems. By one estimate, only about 10% of American hospitals even have electronic medical records—those that do, often find their software programs buggy and inadequate.[32] And only an estimated ¼ of primary-care doctors use electronic health records.[33] Many still write their prescriptions by hand, potentially confusing Celexa, Celebrex and Cerebyx. [34]

Hospital professionals, including nurses, pharmacists, lab technicians, orderlies, specialists and others, need up-to-date, accurate information. Absent such dynamic data, 'wrong side' surgery still occurs once every 15,000 operations. And, as the IOM found, hospital patients experience, on average, 1 medication error such as receiving the wrong drug or wrong dosage, every day they stay in the hospital! [35] (This actually happened to my wife twice that we know of, during stays at two different, highly respected Harvard Medical School affiliated teaching hospitals in 2007 and 2008. Once the quite attentive night nurse apologized for giving double the doctor prescribed dosage: 'I misread the chart.' The other time, the harried overnight resident prescribed a nighttime sleeping medication for 8 AM dosage.)

Indeed, Time Magazine reported in 2006 on the three things doctors feared most about becoming a hospital patient: fear of medical errors, fear of unnecessary surgery and fear of contracting a staph infection in a teaching hospital.[36] Total cost to the US economy of these preventable medical errors: $17-$29 billion annually.[37]

Medicare is so upset at hospital safety results that, effective October, 2008, it will no longer pay extra for hospital care needed to remedy a previous hospital mistake. (Prior to this policy announcement—astonishingly—hospitals could get paid twice for the same patient: first to treat the patient, and second to correct the treatment mistakes from the first attempt!). Perhaps as a result Boston's Beth Israel Deaconess Medical Center announced in January of 2008 'an ambitious quality-improvement effort aimed at eliminating within four years all harm to patients that it considers preventable, such as falls, infections caused by intravenous lines, and medication errors.'[38] I wonder why they allowed preventable harm to patients previously?

Hospital safety problems are, and have been for years, solvable. The US Veterans Administration, for example, has already solved many of them in its hospital network. [39] Unfortunately, few private hospitals or insurance carriers have found that addressing them is economically attractive.

The reason: Development of an efficient information technology system, or hospital-wide safety system, is expensive, requiring a long time to recoup the investment. The first hospital that so develops will increase its overhead—and likely lose money, based on the DRG reimbursement formula. The first carrier to so develop will increase its overhead—but likely be unable to increase premiums sufficiently (without losing customers) to recoup the investment. In short, the current US healthcare system provides little incentive for major investments in IT or safety.

Because of this underlying incentive structure, the Institute of Medicine bluntly states that 'reform around the margin is inadequate to address system ills.' The Institute seems to invite discussion of major overhaul options for the American healthcare system.

Let's return to our six systemic issues that define a well functioning healthcare system. Such a system would have

1. A low rate (or no) uninsured people;
2. Little or no medical arms race but good access to care;
3. Little or no moral hazard systemic waste;
4. Good chronic disease and preventive care;
5. Standard, evidence-based treatments; and
6. High quality, safe medicine

We'll examine various systemic options and proposals to improve the US healthcare system in light of these 6 criteria.

CHAPTER 5
Pro-Single Payer Arguments

This chapter summarizes the 5 main pro-single payer arguments: (1) the Overhead Argument, (2) the Equity Argument, (3) the Uniformity of Treatment Argument, (4) the Guild Argument and (5) the Incentive Argument.

Proponents of Single Payer Healthcare (sometimes also called Universal Healthcare) generally begin with three facts about the current US healthcare system:

1. We have about 45 million uninsured Americans;
2. Our healthcare costs more than any other country; and
3. Our health outcomes as measured by obesity, longevity and infant mortality are mediocre by international standards.

Authors typically discuss problems encompassed by these three points and then conclude that the US should switch to a single payer healthcare system. Authors typically do not discuss the following issues in much depth, if at all:

1. How to switch from our current system;
2. How the current economic incentives and rewards will change;
3. Consequences of altering the incentive and reward structure of 15% ($2 trillion) of our economy;
4. How our historical experience and value structures will interact with single payer social philosophy.

Eloquent arguments that our current system is dysfunctional do not logically or necessarily lead to the conclusion that 'we need a single payer system.' The only arguments that so conclude are those that evaluate single payer systems on their merits.

A word of caution before proceeding: Single payer systems vary. US Medicare—a single payer system—exhibits financing features that the Veterans' Administration Healthcare system does not. Canadian medicare varies from the British National Health Service. The fact that one single payer system presents certain problems does not necessarily indicate that all do.

ARGUMENTS SUPPORTING SINGLE PAYER HEALTHCARE

Argument #1: The Physicians for a National Health Program Plan. The Physicians for a National Health Program (PNHP), a leading proponent of single payer healthcare, argues that a single payer system would reduce overhead drastically and insure the uninsured. The core PNHP position summary:[1]

1. Our current patchwork system has enormous overhead costs—underwriting, billing, sales and marketing, which include huge profits and exorbitant executive pay;
2. Doctors and hospitals must maintain costly administrative staffs to deal with bureaucracy;
3. Approximately 1/3 of American healthcare dollars go toward overhead;
4. By eliminating this unnecessary overhead, a single payer system can save $300 billion or more annually.

On February 4, 2003, a PNHP proposal was adapted into legislative form by Congressmen John Conyers, Dennis Kucinich and Jim McDermont as HR 676 'The US National Health Insurance Act.' Dr. Marcia Angell, Harvard professor and former editor of the New England Journal of Medicine, made a statement at the introduction ceremony.[2] Her statement reads almost like a Declaration of Healthcare Independence. Here's a summary:

The United States is the only developed country with 40+ million uninsured. We rank poorly on international scales of infant mortality, life expectancy and immunization rates. Canadians, on the other hand, spend much less on healthcare and see doctors more frequently; Canada has a single payer system.

US health insurance carriers are 'mostly investor-owned, for profit managed care businesses'. They keep premiums down and profits up by stinting on medical services or not insuring expensive subscribers. That makes us the 'only nation in the world with a health care system based on dodging sick people.'

The US medical cost structure: First, carriers take 10-25% of premium for administrative overhead. The remainder goes to 'satellite businesses that feed on the healthcare industry'—brokers to cut deals, disease-management and utilization review companies, drug management companies, legal services, marketing consultants, billing agencies, IT firms and others. 'Their function is often to limit services in one way or another...I would estimate that no more than 50 cents on the healthcare dollar actually reaches the providers—who themselves face high overhead costs in dealing with multiple insurers.'

The Physicians for a National Health Plan proposal is 'the very soul of simplicity and efficiency compared with out private health care system.' A single, public entity pays all medical costs. Healthcare is coordinated to eliminate gaps and overlap. This proposal is 'tantamount to extending Medicare to the entire population...by far the most efficient part of our health care system, with overhead costs of less than 3 percent, and it covers virtually everyone over the age of 65.'

Dr. Angell then discusses the standard objections or 'myths' associated with single payer healthcare:

Myth #1: National healthcare is unaffordable and will lead to rationing. 'We can't afford not to have a national health care system,' she says. Such a system would be far more efficient by eliminating excess administrative costs, profits, cost-shifting and unnecessary duplication. Indeed, a single payer healthcare system would establish 'an overall budget and the fair and rational distribution of resources."

Myth #2: Single payer healthcare would reduce technological innovation, have long waiting lists and a general reduction in medical care. This myth is based on experiences in Canada and Britain—both of which spend far less on healthcare than us. 'If they were to put the same amount of money as we do into their system, there would be no waits and all their citizens would have immediate access to all the care they need...For them, the problem is not the system; it's the money. For us, it's not the money; it's the system.'

Myth #3: A single payer system is socialized medicine with it's own onerous bureaucratic regulations. But that's not the case with Medicare. 'Nothing could be more onerous both to patients and providers than the multiple, intrusive regulations imposed on them by the private insurance industry.'

Myth #4: The government can't do anything right. But the National Institutes of Health, the National Park Service and the Internal Revenue Service all work quite well.

In conclusion, Dr. Angell says that our disparities in income, material possessions and social privilege 'should not extend to denying some of our citizens certain essential services because of their income or social status. One of those services is healthcare. Others are education, clean water and air, equal justice and protection from crime...Providing these essential service to all Americans, regardless of who they are, helps insure that we remain a cohesive and optimistic country.'

Other PNHP statements add details to Dr. Angell. Their <u>Proposal of the Physicians' Working Group for Single-Payer National Health Insurance</u> [6] lists four principals that shape their vision of reform.

1. Access to comprehensive healthcare is a human right. Coverage should not be tied to employment. 'Private insurance firms' past record disqualifies them from a central role in managing healthcare.'
2. 'The right to choose and change one's physician is fundamental to patient autonomy.'
3. The pursuit of corporate profit and personal fortune has no place in care giving and they create enormous waste. The US already spends enough to provide comprehensive healthcare to all Americans with no increase in total costs.'
4. 'In a democracy, the public should set overall health policies. Personal medical decisions must be made by patients with their care givers, not by corporate or government bureaucracies.'

The **Proposal** continues that a single, public plan will cover all medically necessary services for all Americans, with no copayments or deductibles. 'Boards of expert and community representatives would assess which services are unnecessary or ineffective and exclude them from coverage.'

The National Health Insurance would pay each hospital a monthly lump sum to cover all operating expenses; hospitals would not bill for services. Capital expenditures, expansion, capital purchases or leases 'would be appropriated separately based upon community needs... Investor-owned hospitals would be converted to not-for-profit status and their owners compensated for past investment.'

'These methods of hospital payment would shift the focus of hospital administration away from lucrative services that enhance the bottom line and toward providing optimal clinical services in accord with patient's needs.'

Private health insurance that duplicates this national program would become illegal, as it will undermine the public system.

This insurance program would save at least $150 billion annually[7] by eliminating unnecessary overhead and profits. 'During the transition to an NHI, the savings on administration and profits would fully offset the costs of expanded and improved coverage. NHI would make it possible to set and enforce overall spending limits for the healthcare system, slowing cost growth over the long run.'

This type of argument raises several fundamental questions. **First**, it looks like the utopian social engineering process that Karl Popper described. The PNHP wants to impose its values on the whole of American society and transform the nature of Americans. Its immodest blueprint aims to control both our social and medical system evolution. This is impossible, according to Popper, as there are far too many variables for the PNHP plan to control—- leading to a hodge-podge of unplanned solutions to unanticipated problems.

Second, if healthcare inflation continues at approximately 10%/ year (as it has since about 2000), then the 30% savings from overhead reduction will disappear in 3 years. In other words, 3 years from now our healthcare costs will approximately equal today's and healthcare inflation will continue unchecked, for the PNHP proposal does not provide a long-term, sustainable cost-control and quality improvement structure.

Third, choosing Medicare as the model for national health insurance finance opens a Pandora's box of equity and efficiency issues. We'll discuss these more in the Medicare chapter.

Fourth, capitating hospital payments, similar to the British National Health Service, controls costs primarily through service <u>denial</u>. Budget forecasting errors early in the payment cycle for example, may result in service denials later in the cycle, as happened in North London hospitals in 2006. We'll discuss this in detail in Chapter 8.

Fifth, no proposal that reorganizes the incentive and reward structure of 15% of the US economy call justifiably be called 'the very soul of simplicity': there are lots of economic repercussions and consequences. Let's guess at a few:

<u>**Technological innovation.**</u> The PNHP proposals aim directly at reducing the medical arms race, for local community boards—not the market—would determine which hospitals invest in which specialties and technologies. Would some communities decide <u>not</u> to purchase the newest available technologies? How would their citizens respond? Unclear. (This might simply recreate the medical arms race, but this time pit community against community, rather than hospital against hospital. Or it might not.)

Would this process result in fewer new medical technology purchases nationally? Also unclear. But if so, how would this affect Wall Street's interest in funding biomed or other medical technologies? Again, unclear.

A reduction in demand for medical technologies might reduce financing available for new technologies. That could affect the future domestic growth both of biotech and other industries. How would that affect us? How would that affect our foreign competitors? Could that affect our balance of payments? Could there be other effects? Unknown at this time. But worth considering.

<u>**Self-selection of medical professionals.**</u> Eliminating the 'pursuit of personal fortune' from caregivers may alter the population that enters the medical field. Will this improve care, as only those with entirely noble values will enter? Or will care suffer, as the best and the brightest seek their fortunes in other fields? Unclear.

<u>**Reduction in home values.**</u> If thousands of insurance carrier employees and hospital financial administrators suddenly lose their jobs, many may be unable to continue paying their monthly mortgages. Would they get similar jobs at similar pay quickly? Unknown. The resulting foreclosures might decrease property values. How would this affect the US economy, banking system or local government tax collections? Unclear. Could this affect local school funding and lead to teacher layoffs? Unclear. But possibly.

This is <u>not</u> an argument for maintaining highly paid insurance executives to the detriment of our healthcare system. It <u>is</u>, however, an argument for thinking through the effects of altering our healthcare reward system.

American politics. Currently the health insurance and hospital lobbies play significant roles in State and Federal government. How would loss of these interest groups affect politics and legislation? Unclear.

Possibly groups that currently lobby against the insurance and hospital industries would benefit. Or, possibly, other groups might benefit more; healthcare lobbyists with their contacts, abilities and clout could shift their efforts to promoting other industries. Absent insurance and hospital political interests, others might have easier access to the political process…affecting our political system in currently unanticipated ways. Could this happen? Possibly.

The PNHP argument seems overly simple and poorly thought-through. It may be valid—but absent a clear and cogent discussion of effects, ripple effects and consequences, this argument looks simplistic and weak.

Argument #2: The Equity Argument. The PNHP and others sometimes argue that all Americans should have the <u>same</u> health insurance program. This would build national cohesion and provide other social benefits. As Drs. Rashi Fein and Julius B. Richmond state: "We believe that the most effective, efficient, and equitable health care insurance system would be…'single payer' ". [8]

Dr. Angell also supports this position by claiming 'only a single comprehensive program, covering rich and poor alike, can end disparities based on race, ethnicity, social class and geographic region…'[9]

Proponents sometimes state this argument as follows: Equality is fundamental in our society. All Americans are entitled to equal justice under law, equal opportunities for advancement, equal access to clean air and water, equal access to credit, equal opportunities to vote and many other types of equality. Healthcare is another social good that we should all access equally. Single payer healthcare offers that structure; other types of healthcare financing do not.

This position equates 'same health insurance' with 'equal access to treatment' and raises an empirical question: do people living in countries with single payer healthcare actually have equal access to treatment?

Phrased differently, if there are any healthcare resource constraints, do single payer systems distribute the available resources equally?

The evidence clearly says no, that in single payer systems

> Not only is access to healthcare not equal, if anything it tends to correlate with income—with the middle class getting more access than the poor and the rich getting more access than the middle class....these systems tend to overspend on the relatively healthy while denying the truly sick access to specialist care.[10]

This problem is endemic to the single payer structure because wealthy and politically well connected people always get better services than the poor. In Britain, for example, the wealthiest areas around London have the highest ratio of medical services per capita while poorer sections of, for example Scotland, have far lower. This has led the British press to refer to the 'postcode lottery' in which a person's chances of receiving timely, high quality treatment depend on the neighborhood or 'postcode' of residence, due to geographic specialist referral restrictions.[11]

A specific example: 49% of British hemodialysis facilities are located in (wealthy, politically powerful) London and southeastern England— home to only 25% of the population. Dialysis patients living in this relatively small geographic region have 3x easier access to dialysis facilities than the 75% of the population living elsewhere in England, Scotland, Wales and Northern Ireland—without even considering travel distances or available public transportation (better near London).[12]

Another example: The 'Good Hospital Guide' grades every hospital in Britain on a mortality index and finds that hospitals in wealthy sections of London rated highest on patient mortality scales, while hospitals in the poorest sections rated lowest. London's top 10 hospitals ranked by mortality, and all in wealthy postcodes, average 52 physicians/100 beds, while the 10 worst (in poor postcodes) average only 31 physicians—a 40% difference! [13]

Canadian MRI machine distribution follows the same pattern. Wealthy and politically powerful Ontario had in 2001 approximately 11,900,000 inhabitants [14] and 53 MRI machines [15] for a machine/ inhabitant ratio of 4.4 (normalizing the ratio by multiplying by 1,000,000). Large, spread-out Saskatchewan had machine/inhabitant ratio of about 1.0; Manitoba about 0.8. Meanwhile small and relatively unempowered

Nova Scotia, New Brunswick and Newfoundland had average machine/inhabitant ratios under 1.3, as did French-speaking Quebec. The wealthy and powerful in Ontario had about 4x easier/better access to MRI machines than the 1/3 of Canadians living in Saskatchewan, Manitoba, Quebec, Nova Scotia and New Brunswick—even before considering transportation issues.

There is a second definition of equal access also: time. In single payer systems does everyone <u>wait</u> approximately the same amount of time for treatment? Or do the rich and powerful get to specialists more quickly than others?

In Britain, according to a quip about buying private health insurance rather than using the National Health Service: 'You wait to avoid paying or pay to avoid waiting.' One of the main reasons people purchase private health insurance is to 'jump the queue' and get services privately. But who purchases this expensive insurance? The wealthy. In 2000, 11% of the British population owned private health insurance. But this group consisted of 22% of Britons labeling themselves as 'professionals' and 23% as 'employers and managers,' compared with 4% of (relatively poor) Scots.[16]

In addition to queue jumping, private insurance allows you access to your physician of choice because of the National Health Service regulations that limit public access to specialists, both geographically and by referral restrictions. [17]

Even in Canada, where no private health insurance competes with Canadian medicare, the wealthy and powerful still use their connections to access better treatment. Dr. Arnold Aberman, dean of the University of Toronto medical school during the 1990s, explains that 'Three or four times a week, sometimes, I would arrange preferred access to medical care. I wasn't proud of it...because by helping someone I knew, I was hurting someone I didn't know.'[18] People who asked such favors included top bureaucrats and politicians.

'I once got a call from an assistant deputy minister who had twisted her ankle. She asked if I could arrange for her to see an orthopedic surgeon immediately,' which he did. Two weeks later he sat on a panel with her, while she verbalized her pride in the Canadian system where no one can buy his or her way ahead of others. Dr. Aberman said nothing as 'she controlled the money for our medical school'.

Dr. Angell responded to Myth #2 about investments and decreased medical care availability and quality in single payer systems by stating that, 'the problem is not the system, it's the money', arguing that if Britain, Canada and others invested as we do on healthcare then resource constraints would disappear.

But healthcare resources are <u>always</u> somewhat constrained. Even in greater Boston with extensive medical resources, we hear reports of 3 month waits for liver specialist consultations, child psychiatric appointments, dermatology referrals and others. Many primary care physicians have full caseloads, forcing some consumers to scramble to find an available PCP.[19]

The single payer healthcare financing system itself does nothing to promote more equal access to treatments. It simply gives everyone the same access to gatekeepers...and then allows the wealthy and powerful to use their connections to jump the queue and get preferential care. As these examples show (and there are many, many more), in single payer systems the equality problem may be entirely systemic, regardless of availability of money.

This, then, also appears another weak argument for single payer healthcare.

Argument #3: The Uniformity of Treatment Argument. The Dartmouth Medical School researchers, National Committee on Quality Assurance and others have documented significant medical treatment cost and practice variation by region, hospital and specialist. Among the findings:

- Average medical costs/Medicare recipient in Miami are about double that of Medicare recipients in Minneapolis during their last 6 months of life [20];
- The 'disparity between the care most Americans receive and the care delivered through the nation's best plans results in from 42,000 to 79,000 premature deaths each year'[21];
- 'Thousands of preventable second heart attacks, kidney failures and other conditions...could be averted through more consistent delivery of best-practice care'[22];
- The National Center for Health Statistics has concluded that $1 billion/year in physician and hospital charges would be saved if cesareans were performed at the 'optimal' rate of 15% of births.[23]

Single payer proponents claim that establishing a national healthcare system will eliminate these discrepancies because the single payer will dictate treatment processes and practices. This top-down management approach will define 'best practices' for the entire country and sanction providers who fail to follow. Pat and Hugh Armstrong, enthusiastic proponents of the Canadian single payer system claim that as a result of this approach 'our non-profit system is more efficient and effective [than America's] however these are measured.'[24]

We know, for example, that prescribing beta blockers to patients after heart attacks will save lives. But only 86% of hospitals regularly prescribed these in 2003.[25] Similarly, only 49% of providers regularly helped patients control high blood pressure.[26] Single payer proponents claim that absent strong, central practice mandates, these treatment variations will continue at an enormous cost of lives and resources. We need, in other words, clear national regulations that define best practices, to which all providers must adhere.

Economists have raised three questions about this approach. **First**, Medicare—our national single payer system for the elderly and the PNHP's proposed model system—already has over 100,000 pages of regulations and appendices, but still notes significant regional and provider treatment differences. Would more pages of regulations achieve the uniformity of treatment goal? This is unsettling. If you can't achieve uniformity with 100,000 pages of regulation, then perhaps the regulatory approach to uniform treatment quality is inappropriate.

Second, the American Academy of Actuaries has raised concerns about provider compliance bonuses and penalties. Small bonuses may not induce sufficient provider behavioral change, but large bonuses need very careful consideration, for these may stifle innovation and physician creativity and skew provider cash flow unintentionally.[27]

Third, and perhaps most significant, this top-down management approach is about process compliance, not results improvement, and has serious limitations.[28] Medical care is complex and given the many variables and judgements required, it is still possible for providers to have wide variation in outcomes even if they exhibit uniform process compliance. Researchers have found this in treatment of cystic fibrosis, for example.

Michael Porter of Harvard Business School worries that incentives for process conformance rather than outcomes and results are misplaced.

Discrete processes, rather than being the key to best outcomes, are only 'a lowest-common-denominator starting point' as diagnostic judgement plays a bigger part in medical outcomes. There are too many dimensions of process to track and too much heterogeneity among patients for this regulatory activity to succeed. Process compliance ignores the important dimension of how providers work with patients to improve their choices and avoid unnecessary care.

Most process oriented regulations address only those few processes on which consensus has been achieved and have data available. Porter worries that codified treatment process regulations may inhibit innovation and slow the growth of outcome based medical practices. He fears micromanaging hospitals and doctors by specifying processes. Specified processes and process guidelines easily morph into administratively determined medical decisions so administrators, rather than caregivers, specify what care may be and should be provided to patients. This is Michels' point: that healthcare reform ends when administrators take over. Innovation suffers.

Dr. Sherwin Nuland of Yale Medical School agrees:[29]

> 'Better watch out or the pendulum swing of medical dogma will bash your head in. It swings back and forth far more often than most people realize and with far greater velocity. Thirty years ago patients with inflammation of...the colon were routinely treated with a diet low in roughage. There was no uncertainty about this course of action...and yet, a few years later, medical opinion reversed: decreased roughage was found not to be a panacea but a cause of the disease. This new medical discovery was announced in the same assuredness and supported by just as much evidence as had been used for precisely the opposite viewpoint...Clinical theory and decision making are a mix of science, experience, contemporary culture...and even emotion.'

Drs. H Gilbert Welch and Steven Woloshin also agree in a Jan 1, 2008 Boston Globe op-ed piece. They suggest that similar situations existed for hormone replacement in post-menopausal women, bone marrow transplantation in women with breast cancer and stent placement for patients after heart attacks. Porter, Nuland, Welch and Woloshin suggest that outcome improvements, rather than process compliance uniformity, should be medicine's focus. Imposed process uniformity exacerbates, rather than mitigates, the problem of poor quality medicine.

Thus, the uniformity of treatment argument for single payer healthcare also falls short.

Argument #4: The Guild Argument (a.k.a. 'Medicine is Different from Other Economic Activities'). So far we have evaluated single payer healthcare proposals from an economic perspective. But some have argued that healthcare is essentially a different kind of human activity, one that needs a different set of analytic tools. This position is perhaps most clearly stated by Dr. Arnold Relman, a Harvard professor and another former editor of the New England Journal of Medicine.

Physicians sometimes phrase this argument as 'Insurance carriers and regulators interfere far too much with my ability to practice medicine. Just leave me alone so I can use my own training, experience and best judgement to treat my patients. I'm a healer, not a businessman.'

Relman argues that in all other capitalist economic activities the buyer has access to reasonable information about the product or service in question. Medicine is different however, 'since patients usually know little about the technical aspects of medicine and are often sick and frightened [so] they cannot independently choose their own medical service the way that consumers choose most services in the usual market. As a result, patients must trust physicians to choose what service they need...'[30]

Relman believes that we need non-market mechanisms such as professional educational requirements and licensure rather than market economics to protect patients—just like a traditional guild. He questions the equation of medicine with economics by suggesting that 'medical care is not really a "market" at all in the classical economic sense, and therefore...the basic theories of economics are not relevant to the discussion of...healthcare.'

He then shows how economic market failures in healthcare have led to our current mess, noting our landscape of investor-owned insurance companies, investor-owned hospitals, investor-owned ambulatory-care facilities and nursing homes and non-profits that act like investor-owned operations. He notes that American physicians 'to a degree greater than anywhere else in the world...think of themselves as competitive businesspeople' and form investor-owned medical groups that advertise to the public.

Relman wants to remove economic and business concerns from healthcare, thus freeing practitioners from these market constraints. He sees single payer healthcare, with appropriate regulations and medical service reorganization, as the non-market mechanism that will allow highly qualified, trained physicians to reward patient trust by focusing entirely on patient needs. This, he believes, will reduce the number of uninsured Americans and provide better healthcare results at lower costs than today.

He outlines a healthcare system structure comprised of a single funding source, pre-paid, non-profit, multi-specialty group practices with salaried physicians and no competing private health insurance.[31] Physicians would 'more likely employ technology according to accepted standards... [prescribe drugs] in a more rational and conservative manner...[and] adhere to standards that are monitored by their own internal peer-review procedures' than currently.[32] His system would reverse the 'insidious erosion of professional norms and their replacement by business values'. [33]

By suggesting that healthcare is not really an economic market, Relman tries to avoid economic-based criticisms. Indeed, he laments: 'our society assumes that market economics applies to virtually all human activity involving the exchange of goods or services for money, and this dogma is rarely questioned.' He questions that dogma, outlines a new healthcare system, and seeks a different vocabulary and viewpoint from which to discuss healthcare.

Thus pointing out economic problems with his theories falls into 'Relman's Trap'. He may well accept all the economic criticism and respond 'inapplicable'.[34] Economics has an inappropriate language, uses inappropriate measures and has not solved our healthcare problems—it's time to try something else. He claims 'I am convinced that a complete overhaul [to single payer funding] is inevitable, because in the long run nothing else is likely to work.' The reason: healthcare is essentially different from all other economic activity, more appropriate for a guild-like structure than economic competition.

Unfortunately, 500 years or so of market economics has given us a particular shared mindset and vocabulary to discuss resource distribution and allocation; guilds collapsed historically due to mercantile competition and their lack of ability to innovate.

Relman's Trap only goes so far: if he rules out economics as a tool to discuss healthcare, he must then provide his own tools, language, measures or indicators. This he has not done—he merely describes his vision of a better healthcare delivery system structure. How would we know that his system works? He fails to provide a language or vocabulary to discuss this. What are his units of measure if indeed we can measure his new system—physician trust? Patient satisfaction? Provider satisfaction? How does his system deal with constraints, resource allocations, bottlenecks and excess demand? And perhaps most importantly, how does his system innovate? Professional educational requirements and licensure regulations—i.e. guild entry requirements—are notoriously conservative and change-resistant instruments. This seems to contrast with medicine's constantly increasing pace of innovation.

Relman's messianic conviction about a complete system transformation falls beneath Popper's criticism of utopian social engineering. His proposals seek to transform not only our healthcare system, but also the 'nature of man'—apparently by returning to the social values and social consciousness of an earlier era, or perhaps to his view of human nature based on his personal value structure. He ignores the evolution of American society as he wants to eliminate profits, private insurance, market mechanisms and various choice options from American healthcare consumers. Perhaps in another time or place his proposals would be successful.

But today his position disappoints. From his potentially interesting questioning of economic dogma, he degenerates simply to showing flaws in our current healthcare system and his vision of the future. His utopian vision seems grounded more his own personal philosophy than in the social values currently prevalent in America. He tacitly admits this by recognizing that the short term political prospects for his system are not very good since they are out of line with current American thinking.

We are no longer the America of an earlier era—the era before hospitals and carriers became privately owned, before technology led to great medical advances, before the hospital sector became an economic power, before private health insurance became a way of life, before healthcare consumers demanded wide provider choice. Interestingly, Britain initiated its National Health Service in such a time (1942), and Canada also before their physician, hospital and the private medical sectors were nearly as developed as ours are today.

By failing to tie his vision of healthcare systemic improvements to current American political and social values, Relman seeks to transform the nature of both American society and mankind. As Popper has devastatingly shown, this attempt at utopian social engineering cannot be successful.

Argument #5: The Incentive Argument. The incentive argument for a single payer healthcare system starts with Relman's initial point: that medicine is different from other economic markets. Consumers ally themselves with practitioners who provide diagnoses, advice and treatment. Healthcare consumers shop differently from, for example, automobile consumers, as consumers cannot access objective provider quality data. Therefore, provider trust plays a key role in healthcare, unlike other economic markets.[35]

Financial incentives may affect physician judgement and lead physicians, often under carrier pressure, to abuse this trust relationship. Providers and carriers might consider factors other than long term patient health when designing treatments. What are some of these factors?

First, providers might consider current insurance carrier reimbursement categories, such as DRGs, and design treatment plans around reimbursements rather than patient need. **Second,** providers might consider their own bonus situation—perhaps they receive a bonus only if they refer to a particular specialist network or hospital. **Third,** as we discussed in the Manhattan Beth Israel Medical Center section of Chapter 4, providers may implement short term solutions to long term problems.

And **fourth,** our current healthcare system rewards specialists more lucratively than primary care physicians. As a result, America has proportionally more specialists and fewer primary care doctors than any other country.

Phillip Longman in <u>Best Care Anywhere</u> [36] a case-study of the Veterans Administration Healthcare System, discusses how a single payer system can alleviate these problems and work more effectively in patient's long term interests.

The VA single payer system, for example, has a lifetime relationship with its enrollees, creating an incentive for investing in prevention and effective chronic disease treatments. 'If you know you're going to have your patients for five years, ten years, 15 years or life, there are both good economic and health reasons why you would want to [make certain decisions]' according to Dr. Kenneth Kizer, former VA Undersecretary for Health.

You would, for example, choose a drug formulary with lower long term costs and better long term patient results, even if the short term costs were higher.

You would invest more money up-front in a first-class hospital IT system, knowing that you will have a high return on investment over the long term, though not necessarily the short.

You would also invest more in hospital safety programs, knowing that the long term payback is very good.

And, perhaps most significantly, the long term incentives promote good preventive healthcare—perhaps the single most egregious failing of our current healthcare system.

Appropriate long term incentives would eliminate several systemic factors currently plaguing American healthcare, described in Chapter 4. Chronic disease care would improve, hospital safety would improve, moral hazard might shrink and patients could access real, effective preventive medicine.

The US Veterans Administration Healthcare System provides an example of how a long term perspective can lead to an efficient, effective healthcare delivery system. The VA, with it's long term patient time horizon, has developed perhaps the world's best medical IT and safety systems, generated better outcome results than private hospitals and controlled costs more effectively than our national market-based healthcare system.[36]

This is an extremely strong argument. A healthcare system with appropriate long term incentives will almost certainly outperform a healthcare system with using only short term. A system designed around appropriate incentives would likely exhibit better results at lower costs. The questions:

Can we fashion a well functioning healthcare system around appropriate long term incentives?

Must long term incentives mean single payer financing, or can we use long term incentives in any other type of health insurance?

We'll explore attempts to implement such a system in case studies of Canadian medicare, the British National Health Service, US Medicare and the US Veterans Administration healthcare system.

But first, let's summarize this chapter and relate single payer theory to our 6 underlying healthcare problem areas.

1. <u>The Uninsured</u>: A national single payer system would insure everyone. This is perhaps its strongest point.

2. **The Medical Arms Race**: There is little in the PNHP proposals or Relman's theory to indicate that the Medical Arms Race would disappear. Each physicians group, hospital or locality would decide independently which technologies to purchase—much like today. Medicare's reimbursement practices in particular—the PNHP's proposed model system—exacerbate the Medical Arms Race. See Chapter 9.

3. **Moral Hazard**: An efficient single payer system may reduce the rate of moral hazard, as physicians might lose some incentives to overtreat patients. Consumers could still overburden the system with demands for questionable or unnecessary treatment, absent some form of rationing. Depending on a number of factors—including tort reform and diagnostic clarity—physicians could continue to waste resources by overtreating, or misallocate resources by treating inappropriately. Two questions to consider: how does a proposed single payer system differentiate between acute, chronic and unnecessary interventions? How should it?

4. **Ineffective Chronic Disease Care and Prevention**: The long term incentive structure discussed by single payer proponents may work to improve our chronic disease care situation as exhibited by the VA. Or it may not, as exhibited by Medicare.

5. **Uneven Treatment Quality Nationwide:** Unclear how a single payer system will deal with this problem. Perhaps a top-down management approach would work; perhaps this would stultify physicians. The VA example suggests that the uneven treatment quality problem is best solved by improved information systems not management control systems.

6. **Relatively Low Quality and Safety Investment**: A single payer system may allow providers to invest more aggressively in information technology and safety systems, depending on the exact reimbursement method. With constrained resources or a poorly planned system, quality and safety levels may remain about where they are today. With adequate financing and good planning, these problems may improve.

Let's turn now to a discussion of problems with single payer financing.

CHAPTER 6
Anti-Single Payer Arguments

This chapter discusses 5 problems with single payer healthcare: (1) Life Expectancy as an indicator of healthcare system efficacy, (2) Waiting Lists, (3) Effects and Outcomes, (4) Innovation and (5) General Hospitals.

A rguments in favor of single payer healthcare generally come in the following form:

- Countries with single payer systems—such as Canada and Britain—have lower healthcare expenses than we do;
- Most developed countries with single payer systems—such as Canada and Britain—have longer life expectancies than we do;
- Therefore we should switch to a single payer healthcare system.

Is life expectancy a valid indicator of healthcare system efficacy?

The Canadian National Forum on Health in 1997 [1] suggests

'We have known for some time that the better off people are in terms of income, social status, social networks, sense of control over their lives, self-esteem and education, the healthier they are likely to be...We know that there is a gradient in health status, with health improving at each step up the slope of income, education and social status.'

The Ontario Premier's Council on Health Strategy [2] listed in order the five most important factors determining good health and longevity:

Social environments: 'People with more social contacts and friends tend to live longer than those with fewer...The lifespan and the health of an individual is linked to his or her location in the job hierarchy and associated with factors such as degree of authority, freedom to make decisions and level of social support in the workplace.'

Physical environments: such as nutrition, food quality, sanitation and environmental cleanliness.

Psychological environment: 'There is growing evidence that mental health influences physical well-being although the exact pathways...are not yet clear.' New research is beginning to explain 'the biological pathway linking social and environment factors with the performance of the immune system and hence the health status of individuals.'

Productivity and wealth: 'Greater wealth is associated with greater health: poorer and middle income people appear to be more vulnerable than wealthy people to a variety of ailments...When socio-economic differences are narrowed, population health status improves.'

The Healthcare system: 'Since the traditional medical care system concentrates on the treatment of ill health...it can only make a limited contribution to the prevention of illness by nurturing overall good health.'

The Canadians suggest that good health and longevity are more influenced by social and environmental factors than the healthcare system. American single payer proponents agree. Drs. Richmond (former US Surgeon General) and Fein (Professor, Harvard Medical School) for example claim that a growing professional census holds that the various US health gains since the 1950s are primarily a result of applying knowledge of health promotion and disease prevention throughout society rather than improved clinical care.[3]

Canadian single payer proponents agree: 'there is clear evidence that the significant overall improvements in health and longevity were primarily the result of improvements in sanitation, housing, nutrition, working conditions, and income distribution' according to Pat and Hugh Armstrong.[4]

These conclusions seem to delegate 'the healthcare system' to a fairly specific function: curing the sick. A thorough discussion of 'the healthcare system' perhaps should include more about social and environmental issues than medical. That, unfortunately, is outside the scope of this particular book.

If life expectancy is not a valid measure of a country's healthcare or medical system, then what is? I suggest that <u>access to appropriate care when necessary</u> is better. Physicians and hospitals can do little to control a patient's social, physical or psychological environments, nor much to increase his/her productivity and wealth. Healthcare providers can, however, do a great deal to heal the sick...but this requires access to appropriate facilities on a timely basis.

Waiting Lists and Resource Allocations:

'Whenever national health insurance has been tried, rationing by waiting is pervasive' claims John Goodman of the National Center for Policy Analysis.[5] This is because single payer systems <u>never</u> fully fund their healthcare systems. Paul McDonald explains why in 'Waiting Lists and Waiting Times for Healthcare in Canada, 1998' (single payer systems publish these kinds of reports; the American healthcare system does not):

> Waiting is widely associated with publicly funded healthcare systems:
> it indicates the absence of costly excess capacity.[6]

National, single payer healthcare systems compete for funds with all other publicly funded activities: defense, education, transportation, environmental control, social security, etc, etc. All these services always want more money for there is always greater need than available resources. (Were the public sector to fully fund all activities the high tax rate would be politically unpopular and economically non-viable.) Healthcare gets its fair share—determined partially by medical need, partially by resource availability and partially by competing needs.

In this necessarily resource constrained healthcare system, how do single payer systems allocate their resources? National healthcare programs 'tend to overspend on the relatively healthy while denying the truly sick access to specialist care and lifesaving medical technology,' says Goodman.[7] This is for political reasons, in an attempt to keep the masses—who are generally healthy—happy. Remember that about 80%+ of the population is relatively healthy and probably more concerned about its tax rate than medical specialist availability. For this group, easy access to primary care and emergency rooms is good politics.

Thus in Canada, over half the physicians are General Practitioners (Primary Care Physicians); in New Zealand, almost half and in Australia almost 2/3. The lack of specialists is apparently a political decision: that it is more important to maintain the existing tax rates / economic status than to allow easy access for all sick people to specialists.

Studies have shown that Canadians visit their primary care doctors about as often as Americans [8] but wait an average 8.3 weeks to see a specialist.[9] The median time in 2003 to see an orthopedic specialist, however, was 13.3 weeks for initial consultation, followed by a median additional wait of 18.9 weeks for treatment, for an average total orthopedic specialist wait of almost 8 months. Uncounted are waits for second opinions.

Waiting list data is sometimes manipulated to show a national healthcare system most attractively. The British National Audit Office, for example, reports that many health authorities make 'inappropriate adjustments' to reduce apparent waiting list times. The official government report title: Inappropriate Adjustments to NHS [National Health Service] Waiting Lists.[10] Just imagine such a report in America!

Some post-2000 waiting examples in Britain:

- 20% of colon cancer cases are considered curable at the time of diagnosis but incurable at the time of treatment;[11]
- Roughly the same situation exists for lung cancer patients in Glasgow;[12]
- 25% of British cardiac patients die while waiting their turn to receive treatment;[13]
- 1 in 6 people on NHS waiting lists for elective surgery are removed without ever being treated.[14]

The Commonwealth Fund generated international medical service wait comparisons in 2002.[15] They looked at the percentage of all adult surgery patients receiving elective (non-emergency) surgery in the previous 2 years, and quantified the number waiting more than 4 months (remember that 'elective' procedures may alleviate painful, debilitating or disabling conditions):

Country	Percent Waiting More than Four Months
Australia	23%
New Zealand	26%
Canada	27%

UK	36%
US	5%

Why do single payer systems skimp on expensive services to the seriously ill while providing so many inexpensive services to the marginally sick? 'Because the later services benefit millions of people (read: millions of voters), while acute and intensive care services concentrate large amounts of money on a handful of patients (read: small number of voters)' according to Goodman.[16]

This also highlights why single payer systems typically charge nothing (no copayment or deductible) at the point of service. These policies cause systemic inefficiencies, moral hazard and bed congestion. Here's why: copayments and/or deductibles reduce unnecessary usage according to numerous studies of healthcare consumption. The classic National Health Insurance Experiment conducted by the Rand Corporation during the 1970s concluded: [17]

1.   Participants who paid for a share of their healthcare used fewer health services than those who did not;
2.   Cost sharing did not significantly affect the quality of care received;
3.   Cost sharing in general had no adverse effects on participant health.

By trying to appease the masses and eliminate copayments for all (read: voters), single payer systems open themselves to moral hazard types of waste—estimated as high as 30% of American healthcare costs. Their only waste control mechanism: the blunt waiting lists that do not differentiate chronic from acute or wasteful physician visits.

However chronic users—repeat customers—may know how to game the system better than acute patients—new customers. The result according to Goodman: as 'these systems leave rationing choice up to local bureaucracies…[they typically] fill hospital beds with chronic patients while acute patients wait for cure.'[18]

This raises important social value questions: should society protect its economic resources and <u>limit</u> healthcare spending? Or should society decide that all patients are entitled to all care, regardless the economics? What social values does the national healthcare financing system express?

There is no clear, simple answer that is universal in time and common to all countries. The Canadians and British, for example, seem to have made their own clear social decision: they will maintain economic stability and limit medical spending and services. Some—a fairly small number of people—will receive sub-optimal care. But society in general will benefit financially.

Remember that about 5% of the population consumes about half the healthcare. Single payer systems have, in effect, decided to protect the interests of the remaining 95% or so. This is a clear, presumably rational and reasonable resource allocation decision for them.

Americans have, to date, rejected this value structure. We believe that each patient should receive all care, regardless the price. One result: we spend more for sick people than single payer countries. Are we right? Are we more compassionate? Or are we being economically foolish? That is up to us to decide based on our shared social values.

Effects and Outcomes:

The same single payer economic theory that limits specialists also limits technology investment. Americans have far easier access to high technology medical equipment and procedures than Britons, Canadians or others. Here is data from the 2002 OECD Databook: [19]

Country	MRI Machines/ Million pop	CT Scanners/ Million pop
US	8.1	14
England	3.9	7
Canada	2.5	8

Effects of this long-term, low investment in specialists and technology in Canada and Britain include both reduced access to tests and treatments and low disease survival rates. In British Columbia, for example in 1999, angioplasty was available in only 1 regional hospital compared to 80% of hospitals in Washington and Oregon. Cardiac catheterization, similarly, was available in 20% of BC hospitals but 90% of Washington and Oregon facilities.[20]

The British have documented a very low survival rate for victims of lung cancer and heart disease specifically due to the underinvestment in medical technology.[21]

The Commonwealth Fund compared incidence and outcomes of breast cancer and prostate cancer internationally.[22] Cancer incidence is largely a function of lifestyle (diet, exercise, stress, smoking), genetics and screening. Mortality rates measure the percentage of those diagnosed that die of the disease. Outcomes are largely a function of early detection and available treatments.

Country	Breast Cancer Incidence/ 100,000 females/year	Breast Cancer Mortality Rates
UK	74	46%
Canada	103	28%
US	111	25%

Country	Prostate Cancer Incidence/ 100,000 males/year	Prostate Cancer Mortality Rates
UK	49	57%
Canada	110	25%
US	136	19%

Goodman summarizes:

> Countries with single-payer health insurance limit healthcare spending by limiting supply. They do so primarily by imposing global budgets on hospitals and area health authorities. Often there is a separate budget for high-tech equipment, to make doubly sure that high cost procedures are curtailed.[23]

Can Single Payer Systems Innovate?

Drs. Angell and Relman in the last chapter argued that these spending constraints would not apply to the US, as we already spend enough to ensure an adequate supply of technology and specialists. We already have short waits for specialist visits and treatments and more technology equipment than almost any other country. Why not just adopt single payer financing and allow growth at, say, the rate of inflation? This surely would keep our technologies current, our disease detections early and our consumers satisfied.

Those who study innovation suggest that single payer systems of the type described by the PNHP do not adopt innovative new approaches, improve medical treatments, invent new processes and improve patient care on a consistent basis. Service rationing to preserve low tax rates and economic and political stability is, in the real world, the norm.

Michael Porter of Harvard Business School provides the market structural reason:

> A single payer system create(s) a...monopoly with absolute bargaining power...With the inevitable and irresistible pressure to control its budget, the single payer engage(s) in major cost shifting to providers, suppliers and patients. In time, rationing of services and deterrents to the adoption of innovative new approaches to care (becomes) inevitable, as we have seen in other countries.[24]

The best—although clearly imperfect—historical mechanism for consistent improvement and innovation is a competitive market according to many including Nobel Prize winner Friedrich Hayek. How can we reduce the number of practicing physicians without decreasing medical quality? What should MRI prices be? Can other medical personnel as reliably perform some tasks previously performed by physicians? Where should healthcare R & D focus its efforts? And most importantly, what is the best way to lower the price of US healthcare and improve quality?

Only through trial and error in a competitive arena can we learn answers to these questions. Competition creates tension as suppliers try to improve quality, reduce price, gain market share and learn the best mechanisms to achieve desired results. Competitive tension is uncomfortable, but we have a 500 year history that demonstrates its information gathering effectiveness.

Much of this tension disappears under single payer scenarios. Top down management imposed answers may—or may not—be the most effective and efficient. If hospitals are homogenized non-profits, physicians all salaried government employees and processes all regulated, then the motivations to innovate decrease. Providers begin to look like monopolies, rarely the sources of innovation, but often the source of high cost, low quality products. This is because large, monopolistic type companies have very strong administrative controls. Remember Robert Michels' warnings about administrators taking over innovation and reform movements.

But how, then, do current single payer healthcare systems overseas innovate? The short answer: they outsource their R & D to us! And then assimilate our results—with time delays—into their own operations. We'll see this happen with British kidney dialysis and radiology practices in Chapter 8. We are often the source of new medical technologies, techniques and research—see, for example, the number of Nobel Prize winners in medicine who work in America.

When single payer theorists detail their policy prescriptions, they generally start and end with financing. They discuss appropriate tax or funding mechanisms but rarely, if ever, detail hospital or provider management, probably for two reasons:

1. Financing is so complex and politically difficult that it's a huge topic by itself;

2. Single payer proponents are rarely (ever?) managers. Interestingly, single payer academics often populate schools of public health, while consumer driven academics teach in business schools. Different academic orientations lead to different policy proposals.

Single payer proponents generally assume continuation of our existing hospital and provider networks, though they may prefer a change of ownership or financing.[26]

Should We Build a Single Payer System on Our Existing General Hospital Base?

Many management experts think our General Hospitals are inefficient and detract from healthcare improvements. Harvard Business School Professor Regina Herzlinger explains that like huge conglomerates, general hospitals

> are often clumsy and slow to innovate. They are hard to manage, requiring a torrent of nourishing cash to keep them alive and massive managerial efforts to keep them networked. Worst of all, [general hospitals] may be bad firms, acting to suppress competition [using political, regulatory and legal means to do so]. [27]

The Institute of Medicine has stated that our currently functioning healthcare system, largely general hospital based, does not provide consistently high quality medical care. Since about 2000, hospital prices grew about 6 times faster than utilization without commensurate increases in quality.[28] Hospital mergers since the 1990s have resulted in consolidation, often with 1 or 2 systems controlling most beds in many cities.

In Cleveland, for example 2 hospital systems control almost 70% of all hospital beds; in Grand Rapids Michigan, 1 hospital system controls 70%, and on Long Island New York, 2 systems control over 80%. In North Carolina, only 18 of 100 counties were served by multiple hospital systems in 2000.[29]

Hospitals consolidated to increase their bargaining power against insurance carriers; they now carry huge overheads and wield enormous political and financial clout. They also generally provide almost every medical service possible, in part to protect their strategic position and in part to serve their customers.

Huge hospital size—and the lack of competition—often reduce rather than improve hospital patient's experiences. As the only game in town they may lack the scale and experience to be particularly proficient all procedures (remember the Leapfrog Groups' minimum annual procedure recommendations from Chapter 4) though they may well be excellent at others. With their huge overheads they may have excess capacity, creating utilization and admission pressures (Roemer's Law). General hospitals are also major local employers.

Single payer proponents want to build on these inefficient behemoths and control their expansion / income growth. This poses two critical problems:

1. Without significantly reforming our healthcare suppliers, a single payer system will do nothing to improve healthcare quality; it will only control overhead and costs;

2. If the single payer tries to squeeze general hospital income, hospitals likely will fight back. They consolidated to gain negotiating power over insurance carriers in the 1990s. Presumably they will negotiate hard with the single payer entity also.

    As major employers (and likely the primary local hospital system due to consolidations), general hospitals will likely lobby local politicians for 'exceptions' to single payer cost control mandates, thus creating a Swiss cheese of cost controls.

Alternatively, general hospitals may simply fight any arbitrary cost control mandates. Current (consolidated) general hospital systems are politically and economically much stronger than were, for example, Canadian hospitals when Canada adopted its current single payer system, or British hospitals in 1942.

We cannot anticipate how these struggles will resolve—only that they will occur.

Why Single Payer Healthcare is a Bad Idea:

A national, single payer healthcare system is a bad idea for the following reasons:

1. Single payer systems restrict access to appropriate care for the sick;
2. Single payer systems under-invest in medical specialties and technologies leading to inferior outcomes;
3. Single payer systems will codify treatment processes and reduce medical innovation;
4. By ignoring general hospital inefficiencies, single payer financing will not improve American healthcare quality or decrease the per unit cost.

But the underlying social value question remains. Is my proposed healthcare system yardstick of 'access to appropriate care when necessary' valid? Is high quality care for a small number of very ill people an appropriate national economic investment? Is national 'reasonable access to primary care costing a modest percentage of GDP' a better path?

Answers to these questions depend on our shared values. Americans seem to believe that everyone should have all the medical care they need— as exhibited by our current tort system and Medicare regulations and reimbursement mechanisms. See Chapter 9 for a Medicare discussion.

Canadians or Britons answer these questions differently. The Canadians seem to think that other values—equality of funding, easy primary care access and a shared experience—are more important than systemic efficiency and exceptional treatment for the sick. The British seem to think that economic stability is a more important social value than 'access to appropriate care for all when necessary.' In the next chapter we'll look at Canadian medicare and see how it reflects a unique set of Canadian social values. Then in Chapter 8, we'll do the same for the British National Health Service.

CHAPTER 7
Case Study: Canada

Canada has a single payer system with no competing private health insurance.

'I'm determined to maintain the current public system...because
I believe profoundly that it is the best from the social perspective
and also makes the most economic sense.'
Canadian Health Minister Allan Rock, 2000[1]

C anada has a single payer healthcare system in which virtually all medical care is government paid. Consumers have no copayments, no deductibles and no medical cost sharing. There is almost no private medical insurance that competes with government programs. Canada by the numbers:[2]

In 2003, Canada invested 10% of GDP in healthcare compared to the US 15% and an OECD (Organization for Economic Cooperation and Development—basically the world's 23 developed countries) average of 8.6%.

Canada had 2.1 practicing physicians per 1,000 people compared to the OECD average 2.9, and 9.8 nurses per 1,000 compared to the OECD average of 8.2.

Canada had 2.8 acute beds per 1,000 in 2002 compared to the OECD average 4.1, and 4.5 MRI units per million population in 2003 compared to the OECD average 7.6.

Sixteen percent of Canadian men are obese, compared to 27% of American men. Canadians live an average 80.7 years compared to Americans 77.9.[3]

The Canadian single payer system is jointly funded by Federal and Provincial (or Territorial) governments. The Feds set mandates and the Provinces implement. The approximate 2004 public system funding: [4]

> Federal government 4%
> Provinces and territories 64%
> Municipal government 1%
> Social security 1%

The remaining 30% comes from the private sector for supplemental services not covered by government healthcare such as dental care, vision care, medical equipment, independent living and services of allied health professionals such as chiropractors and podiatrists.

The 1984 Canada Health Act established the current healthcare system. This Act established the Five Basic Principals of Canadian healthcare: [5]

- **Public Administration:** The provincial and territorial plans must be administered and operated on a non-profit basis by a public authority accountable to the provincial or territorial government;
- **Comprehensiveness:** The provincial and territorial plans must insure all medically necessary services provided by hospitals, medical practitioners and dentists working within a hospital setting;
- **Universality:** The provincial and territorial plans must entitle all insured persons to health insurance coverage on uniform terms and conditions;
- **Accessibility:** The provincial and territorial plans must provide all insured persons reasonable access to medically necessary hospital and physician services without financial or other barriers;
- **Portability:** The provincial and territorial plans must cover all insured persons when they move to another province or territory within Canada and when they travel abroad.

Federal responsibilities include:

- Setting the healthcare agenda and providing financial support;
- Promoting good health and educating the public on health implications of the choices they make;

- Protecting health by regulating food safety, pharmaceuticals, medical devices, consumer products and pest management products;
- Providing funding for health research and health information activities;
- Equalizing healthcare financial payments to less prosperous provinces.[6]

Provincial responsibilities include:

- Administration and delivery of most healthcare services;
- Compliance with the principals of the Canada Health Act;
- Covering medically necessary hospital and doctor's services for free to consumers, without deductibles, copayments or dollar limits;
- Raising sufficient tax revenues to fund their portion.

Private health insurance is legal but under most provincial and territorial laws private insurers are prohibited from offering coverage that duplicates that of the publicly funded plans.[7]

Why did Canadian medicare develop as it did? Dr. David Gratzer, a frequent critic of Canadian healthcare suggests

> The capitalist United States…seemed a dubious, even menacing model to Canadians in the 1960s. It seemed particularly important in an age of rising Canadian self-confidence and national assertiveness to choose policies that would help distinguish the country from market-oriented, anti-Communist, world-dominating America.[8]

(For this type of reason, many Canadians spell medicare with a small 'm' to differentiate it from American Medicare with a capital 'M').

Canada developed its healthcare system to achieve a number of social values, only one of which is 'access to appropriate care when necessary'. Among the other goals:

- Promote equity among Canadians;
- Provide a shared experience for all Canadians;
- Treat healthcare as a public good, with equal access for all Canadians;

- Maintain economic independence and prosperity by controlling healthcare spending, and therefore allow funding of social and environmental programs that promote good health.

Thus a Toronto Star columnist writes 'Canadians understand that a progressive health care system is as much about values as it is about services.'[9]

And the CBC News reports 'Canadians value their medicare as a mark of egalitarianism and independent identity that sets their country apart from the United States.'[10]

How do these values manifest themselves? Canadians have known for years that life expectancy depends on a number of social and environmental factors and want to promote these as well as medicine. The CBC claims that your health depends twice as much on your living situation—education, the environment, etc.—as it does on the medical system.[11] Limiting medical spending allows Canada to invest appropriately in these other important programs.

Janice McKinnon, former Saskatchewan Finance Minister, summarized this in 2005:

> If you look internationally…[medical] spending beyond about $600-$700 US per person per year [shows] literally no correlation between life expectancy, infant mortality and how much you're spending.[12]

Wiser 'healthcare' investments, then, are in education, social infrastructure, environmental safety, nutritional education and the like, rather than in expensive medical technologies.

Why are Canadian obesity levels lower—and life expectancies longer—than American?

Canadians have chosen to make these alternative-type healthcare investments more than Americans. Compare, for example, Ottawa's (population 1 million) 105 miles of publicly maintained bike paths to Houston's (population 2 million) 20. Or see Quebec Province's $88 million investment in 2700 miles of public bike paths during the 1990s. No American region did similarly.

Ferryboats crossing the St. Laurence River in Quebec all have built-in bike racks, but similar boats going to Nantucket, Block Island or Martha's

Vineyard—popular Massachusetts bicycling areas—do not. In these and other examples of social investments, Canadians choose to encourage exercise and healthy activities. These are their real 'healthcare investments.'

The interesting question: why does Canada make such investments while the US does not? The answer: Canada has developed its infrastructure to support its particular zoning and land-use patterns, both quite different from America's.[13]

Canadian cities are generally more densely populated than American with less surrounding suburban sprawl. Canadian metropolitan population densities are about 50% higher than American, while Canadian metropolitan job densities are about 60% higher. As a result, Canadians make shorter—more easily walkable or bikable—work, shopping and pleasure trips from home. Canadians bicycle about twice as much as Americans and walk more than Americans in their normal daily routines.

Canada, consequently, developed a better infrastructure to support these physical types of transportation.

Canadians also own 41% fewer cars and light trucks per capita than Americans. This is due in part to lower Canadian income levels and in part to higher Canadian car ownership and maintenance costs—about 27% higher than American in 2006. One particular element: Canadian gasoline costs about 50% more than American due to higher Canadian gas taxes. Also, car parking in Canada tends to be less available and more expensive than in the US.

These factors led Alain Desroches of the Public Health Agency of Canada to conclude in a personal communication:

> The denser, mixed-used development in Canadian cities leads to average trip distances only half as long in Canada and thus more bikable/walkable than the longer trips Americans make. Canada also has higher transit user rates per capita than US, accounting for walking between trips.

Can these factors affect obesity levels and thus longevity? Let's assume that a 'typical' Canadian walks 5 minutes from home to public transport, then 5 minutes from public transport to work, back and forth each work day. Let's also assume that the typical Canadian walks an additional 20 minutes for shopping, socializing or other routine trips (due to the local availability in high density, mixed use areas) 5 times per week. At 3 miles/hour—a moderate walking pace—this Canadian walks about 500 more miles annually than a similar American.

Walking burns up about 100 calories/mile. Our typical American would need to consume about 50,000 fewer calories per year than this Canadian just to maintain the same weight levels. (This is particularly difficult for the American, especially given the relative availability of high calorie food, using McDonald's franchises as an indicator. McDonald's has about 1 franchise for every 36,000 Canadians versus 1 franchise for every 26,000 Americans.[14])

Other factors, of course, also affect obesity, and we are unsure exactly how 'typical' are these 'typical' Canadians and Americans. Even if, however, other factors mitigate 90% of this analysis, the Canadian still burns 5000 calories more annually than the American. At an average 3500 calories per pound, the American would gain about 1.5 pounds per year more than the Canadian. Extend this for 20+ years and see how American obesity rates exceed Canadian.

If this analysis is valid, we would expect to see two empirical trends. First, Canadian physical activity levels should have increased during the past 20 years while American levels decreased, especially as so many women entered both workforces in the 1980s and 90s. Second, urban Canadians should live longer than rural due to more exercise in their normal daily routines.

The data seems to support these trends. The *Canadian Journal of Public Health* published a 2004 study that analyzed the 20 year trends of physical activity among Canadian adults. The conclusion: levels of physical activity <u>increased</u> in the 1980s and 1990s among Canadians, while these levels <u>decreased</u> among Americans.[15] Canadians walk more— Americans drive more.

Also the *Canadian Institute for Health Information* and *Statistics Canada* published a 2000 report showing that Canadians concentrated in the nation's most densely packed urban areas live the longest.[16] Factors other than routine exercise, of course, may also contribute to this: urban social, physical and psychological environments may be healthier than rural. (See Chapter 6's discussion of the 5 key factors promoting longevity.) But those 500 extra annual walking miles certainly help!

Interestingly, European countries have even denser urban areas with more mixed use zoning than Canada, due largely to their historical development. European countries also have even higher automobile operating costs than Canada, more extensive public transportation and more inviting walking environments. Europeans walk and cycle even more per capita than Canadians, and thus far more than Americans.

Remember Harvard Magazine's description of exercise in Chapter 4's discussion of Ineffective Chronic Disease and Preventive Care: exercise helps prevents heart disease, stroke, diabetes, obesity and 12 kinds of cancer, among other benefits. This provides a context to understand why both Canadians and Europeans live longer than we do even while spending much less on healthcare: they exercise more in their normal daily routines due to their historic zoning, land-use and car usage patterns. They are, consequently, healthier and less demanding of their healthcare systems.

We have argued that Canadians 'healthcare' encompass a wide range of non-medical activities in which Canadians have invested for years. One result: a generally healthier, less obese population than us. Another result: long waits for diagnostic and specialist medical treatment. Some examples:

- Median time to wait for radiation oncology was 9 weeks in 2000.[17] Note that a 6-week delay may mean the difference between a benign tumor metastasizing from the ear into the brain, potentially lethally;
- Five month waits for CT scans in Ontario. 'Waiting lists have become the norm rather than the exception...People are on waiting lists just to get onto other waiting lists' according to Dr. Albert Schumacher, former President of the Ontario Medical Association;[18]
- Canada ranks 12 of 15 developed countries for CT scanners/capita, 11 of 13 for MRI machines, 10 of 11 for kidney and gallstone breakers. It has 2 PET scanners for patients, compared to the US with 250 (for 10x the population).[19] As a result, Canadians waited an average 150 days for an MRI scan in 2001; Americans waited 3;
- Report by the Canadian Association of Radiologists 2000—advised radiologists to tell patients that their diagnosis may be correct at the time of test, but incorrect by the time of treatment. The Report also revealed that up to half of all Canadian radiological machines—from X-ray to CT scanners—are either dilapidated or obsolete;

- 2002 legal opinion solicited by the Canadian Association of Radiologists that advised doctors to inform patients in advance of unreliable and outdated equipment, lest they be sued: 'It is imperative that the patient be advised and understand the risks and uncertainties associated with the reliability of such as examination' advises attorney Chantal Corriveau of Montreal's Jugler Kandestin law firm;[20]
- 27% of Canadians needing non-emergency surgery waited more than 4 months between 2000-2001 compared to 5% of Americans.[21]

Understanding that these waits were unpopular, the government established national wait benchmarks: Hip or knee replacements within 26 weeks, radiation therapy for cancer within 4 weeks, surgery to remove cataracts within 16 weeks for high risk patients, and cardiac bypass treatments within 2—26 weeks, depending on severity. The Canadian Broadcasting Corporation reported in November 2006 the following 'Waiting List Report Card' grades:

Condition	Waiting List Grade
Diagnostic Imaging	F (fewer than half within benchmark)
Joint Replacement	C (60—69% within benchmark)
Sight Restoration	C (60—69% within benchmark)
Cardiac Care (Bypass)	C (60—69% within benchmark)[22]

But Canadians ask a difficult cost-benefit analysis question regarding purchase of expensive medical technologies and investment in expensive medical specialists: do we get a higher social and economic return (however measured) by investing millions in CT scanners or in environmental and exercise programs? Should we put our money into prevention or detection/treatment?

A CT scanner will pick up a few more, small, cancers than X-rays or ultra sound. This early detection will save a few lives, but likely very few; the Commonwealth Fund data discussed in Chapter 6 indicates that all the additional US medical technology only decreases breast cancer mortality by about 3% in the US versus Canada. Is this benefit worth the cost?

Canadians apparently say no. Rather than buying another CT scanner, investing millions in nutritional programs could prevent a large number of children from becoming obese, or in public transportation programs could encourage more walking and bike riding.

Canadian officials have historically chosen these types of investments. Their healthcare, and indeed social and environmental systems reflect these values and the single payer structure allows for these investment choices. So pointing out technology investment differentials between the US and Canada is not a criticism: it is, for many Canadians, a desired goal.

Unfortunately, society, the economy and consumer demands have evolved somewhat differently from the expectation. Even though access to MRI machines, CT scanners and specialists may not significantly impact national life expectancy tables, individual Canadian consumers demand such access. To keep up with this consumer demand, provinces have increased medical funding at substantially over inflation for the past decade—including an average 22% increase between 1998—2000.[23]

As both healthcare expenditures and patient waiting times increased, the government funded 3 studies to determine how best to provide health services in the future.

The **Mazankowski Report** of 2002, written for Alberta Province, presented mechanisms to control the spiraling costs of healthcare, about 1/3 of Alberta's budget. Don Mazankowski, former Canadian Deputy Prime Minister concluded:

> Unless we are prepared to change how we fund and how we deliver healthcare services, the health care system of Alberta is not sustainable.

Some key report recommendations:

- Limit coverage, by dropping some government funded services, and establish a mechanism to decide which medical procedures and services should be covered in the future;
- Service guarantee—reduce waiting lists and guarantee access within 90 days of diagnosis;
- Establish electronic medical records; and
- **Allow some private insurance, thus diluting the 'public only' financing.** Mazankowski verbalizes concerns of many Canadians that the stringent 'public only' financing of healthcare has serious drawbacks.

Some of the recommendations were followed, especially the establishment of electronic records. Before proceeding with the others, Alberta chose to wait on two Federal healthcare reports.

The **Senate (Kirby) Report,** released in October 2002, resulted from a 2- year investigation that heard from over 400 witnesses in over 200 hours of testimony. The key recommendation: raise $5 billion in additional taxes to expand hospitals, buy new equipment, recruit doctors and 'do whatever is needed to improve the system.'[24]

Another key recommendation: If a patient cannot receive timely care, the government should pay for out-of-province or out-of-country treatment. Kirby, a Senator from Nova Scotia, issued this warning:

> If these recommendations are not implemented, then a compelling case could be made to prove that private healthcare insurance is needed.

Kirby agrees with Mazankowski's position that Canadian society may have evolved past 'public only' healthcare financing. By end-2002, we have two major reports—one provincial and the other Federal— questioning this exclusive financing arrangement.

The CBC reported that, as of 2005 'Kirby's key recommendations have not been adopted at the federal level.' His 2002 report seems primarily to have opened the door to these discussions.

The Kirby report was overshadowed by the second Federal report, the **Romanow Report,** released in 2003, which slammed shut that door. Written by former Saskatchewan premier Roy Romanow, this report aimed to:

> Engage Canadians in a national dialogue on the future of healthcare and to make recommendations to preserve the long term sustainability of Canada's universally accessible, publicly funded healthcare system.

Romanow philosophically comes from central Canada's prairie socialist tradition; Saskatchewan is famous for this. His personal position from the 2002 interim report: 'I am convinced that the medicare house needs remodeling, not demolishing.' Thus the private health insurance potential raised by Mazankowski and Kirby was off-limits. Among Romanow's key recommendations:

- Raise more money. Romanow recommended $6.5 billion in new funds, primarily from the Feds;

- Expand medicare payment monitoring. Romanow suggested that 'Accountability' become the 6th pillar of Canadian medicare; and
- **Keep the public sector strong by limiting private insurance.** 'One of the most difficult issues with which I have had to struggle is how much private participation within our universal, single-payer, publicly administered system is warranted or defensible.'

Romanow thinks that expanding private insurance is 'fraught with difficulty.' Letting people who can afford to pay 'jump the queue' for tests and procedures and then get back into the public sector is at odds with a principle at the heart of medicare—equality of access.

Here we see values in conflict. Mazankowski and Kirby see access to high quality medical treatment by sick people as their key value. Though they would prefer public financing, they understand that the private sector may generate better results and are willing to allow this. Their goals (values): cost control, access and treatment improvement.

Romanow holds other values—equality and shared experience—more dearly. He insists that public funding is non-negotiable and the only acceptable healthcare financing mechanism. When equity and efficiency values conflict, Romanow chooses equity; Mazankowski and Kirby chose efficiency.

The courts then entered into this value discussion. In June 2005 the Quebec Supreme Court struck down a law that prohibited people from buying private health insurance to cover procedures already offered by the public system stating 'access to a waiting list is not access to care'. The issue: George Zeliotis, a Quebec resident claimed that a 1-year wait for surgery was unreasonable, life threatening and infringed on Quebec Provinces' guarantee of life, liberty and security.

The court agreed, ruling

The prohibition on obtaining private health insurance might be constitutional in circumstances where healthcare services are reasonable as to both quality and timeliness...[but it] is not constitutional where the public system fails to deliver reasonable services.

Three of the 7 judges wanted to declare Canada's national health system unconstitutional. Because of the potential impact of this decision, the ruling was suspended for 18 months.

We do not yet know how this will affect the Canadian healthcare system. Perhaps the Romanow recommendations will fix the waiting list problems to the Court's satisfaction and the existing publicly funded system will continue. Perhaps the Wall Street Journal is right that this ruling will 'upend similar laws in other provinces' and deal a death-blow to single payer, publicly financed healthcare in Canada.[25] Or perhaps a compromise like the Mazankowski or Kirby recommendations will emerge. It's now simply too early to tell.

Let's review the 6 systemic problems that plague American healthcare and see how Canadian medicare stacks up:

1. **Uninsured:** Canadian medicare insures everyone. There is no uninsured problem.

2. **Medical Arms Race:** Canada's issue is lack of technology investment, not excessive technology overinvestment.

3. **Moral hazard:** The Canadian system addresses moral hazard by waiting lists. These do not differentiate between chronic, acute and unnecessary physician visits. Waiting lists are an inefficient mechanism to deal with moral hazard.

4. **Ineffective chronic disease care and prevention:** We have presented little information on Canadian disease treatment protocols. However, when patients face waits for treatment with old or obsolete technologies, treatment efficacy suffers. Canadians do, however, offer very good primary care. This can have a positive impact on chronic care.

    Canadians also have made significant investments in the social / environmental / lifestyle arenas. Their wider definition of healthcare seems to lead to a healthier population and contributes to longer lives than Americans.

5. **Uneven treatment quality nationally.** The treatment variations in Canada appear, at least partially, due to lack of uniform availability of technology.

6. **Relatively low quality and safety investments.** Much of the quality and safety improvement in the US relies on improved information technology systems in hospitals. **Healthcare in Canada** (2004) discussed some safety issues, but without much IT investment. This is probably due to the severe systemic financial constraints. There is little evidence that Canadian hospitals are safer than American.

Canadian medicare evolved in ways unique to Canada and based on shared Canadian values. Can we transplant it and superimpose this system in the US as some single payer proponents want? No. We lack the history and values that inspired and support Canadian medicare—the prairie socialism, the land use patterns and associated public infrastructure, the more closely shared value of equality, the desire to differentiate from the US and the desire to control national medical expenditures. We can't superimpose their finished system without it's evolutionary past; that would be folly.

Just imagine the scene when a US Medicare beneficiary is told to wait 8 months for an MRI. Or when a business owner is told he cannot purchase private insurance for his family or key employees. Americans— today—would not tolerate this. We have evolved to expect choice of provider with virtually immediate access. Our evolutionary past and values suggest that when faced with a (self-perceived) medical crisis, we will expend our private resources to get a solution quickly. We— Americans—do not share the same social values that Health Minister Rock described at the beginning of this chapter.

We also have not made the same social investments as Canada. Our primary care system is less robust, our preventive care system less functional, our physical / environmental system less exercise oriented, our lifestyles less healthy. The Canadian medical system rests on these social infrastructure bases; transplanting their provider network and financial structure without the underlying base would be a half-measure at best, surely resulting in poorer health outcomes for us.

Attempting to superimpose the Canadian system—the result of a uniquely Canadian evolutionary process—in the US falls to Popper's criticism. For this type of system to succeed in America, we would need to transform not just our healthcare delivery system but also the nature of Americans. We would need to 'become Canadian'—embrace their social perceptions, past social investments, values, culture and orientations. Superimposing their finished product cannot be successful. As Popper has shown, such utopian social engineering <u>always</u> fails.

The Canadian healthcare system has evolved and works—more or less well—for Canada. It will continue to evolve as Canadians see fit. The Mazankowski, Kirby and Romanow reports show the current value tensions among Canadians. As these tensions resolve (or don't), their healthcare system will evolve.

But it will evolve differently from ours.

CHAPTER 8
Case Study of the British National Health Service

Britain has a single payer system with competing private health insurance.

While American healthcare consumes about 15% of our GDP and Canada's represents about 10% of theirs, the British National Health Service only consumes about 8% of British GDP—about half as much as us.

The British have longer life expectancies—— 1.5 years longer on average—and lower infant mortality rates than we do. Perhaps their system can offer some lessons.[1]

SOME BACKGROUND

The British National Health Service (NHS) is a single payer system where the government funds healthcare for all Britons. The NHS mantra is 'free at the point of delivery, provided on the basis of need.' Unlike Canada, however, the British allow private health insurance to compete with the NHS. More on this below.

Parliament determines the annual national healthcare budget, then allocates resources by autonomous geographic region. Each region allocates annual resources by provider, with hospitals getting the bulk of funds. And each hospital allocates annual resources by department.

Budgets remain in place for a year, until the next annual budget begins the process all over again. In general each annual budget is a fairly small percentage change (generally increase) over the previous budget.

Hospitals have difficulty growing at much above the annual inflation factor regardless of medical need, hospital specialty or hospital quality for the following reason: the British regional health authorities have, for years, believed that controlling hospital staffing was the best way to control healthcare spending. The regional authorities simply lack the resources to promote huge hospital expansion projects.

Political considerations enter this budgetary process at several points. First, when Parliament sets that annual national budget, healthcare lobbyists complete with other lobbyists for their share. They compete, for example, with educational lobbyists, environmental lobbyists, transportation lobbyists, foreign aid lobbyists, defense lobbyists and others for part of the national budget. Parliament allocates public monies among these various necessary public functions.

Only part of Parliament's consideration includes actual demand for health services. In addition to healthcare demand, Parliament also considers competing needs for public funds, the political power of each lobby and the availability of resources. The final national budget presumably reflects the 'will of the people' rather than demand for specific medical treatments and technology investments.

After the regional authority makes its hospital funding decisions, then each hospital allocates funding by department. Here the political influence of department heads and senior specialists (called 'consultants' in Britain) becomes important. Some commentators refer to this as a 'semi-feudal system' with consultants, rather than hospital administrators controlling the key funding decisions. The nephrology department may have more political clout and savvy than the neurology department and may thus gain at neurology's expense, almost without regard to relative need.

Demand for specialist services is controlled by General Practitioners (GPs)—the British equivalent of our Primary Care Physicians. GPs act both as medical practitioner and budgetary gatekeeper, regulating patient access to specialists. NHS patients (generally, traditionally) can only access certain hospitals and related specialists: neither GP nor consumers have had system wide hospital choice, though this is changing.

In 2004 Britain had 35,000 GPs, averaging 1600 patients each. Ninety percent of all NHS contacts went no further than the GP in the early 2000s. Unlike Americans who commonly 'doctor-shop', the British were traditionally more likely to accept their doctor's judgement. Perhaps this is due to high esteem in which doctors were held, or perhaps a more stratified social system. In any event, British physicians now report that their younger patients are becoming more demanding, like Americans. This rigid referral system—developed over many years—is starting to break down.

The Brookings Institution's Henry Aaron who has studied the NHS extensively, suggests several social / cultural features that differentiate

Britain from the US or Canada. These support the unique development of the NHS and keep it working satisfactorily:[2]

1. The private sector healthcare reforms introduced by Margaret Thatcher and expanded upon by subsequent governments act as a relief valve for healthcare system congestion;
2. A 'residue of authority' enjoyed by physicians and partly based on deference to them as upper-class members of society enables them to restrict referrals and 'persuade patients that aggressive treatment is inappropriate and induce them to accept such bleak news';
3. The British are somewhat more accepting of results than Americans, and less driven by 'don't just stand there, do something';
4. A deep bedrock of support for the egalitarian principles of the NHS sustains support for the system despite limited resources.

In addition, Parliament traditionally has delegated healthcare policy decisions to the NHS and has not micro-managed that process.

In the NHS's capitated funding system, political and financial considerations that may take precedence over GP referrals and upset patients. **The Observer**, a respected British weekly newspaper, reports (November 5, 2006) that

> Thousands of patients are being denied access to hospital consultants because the NHS has set up money-saving management schemes (that) block GPs' referrals...Patients with rheumatoid arthritis, knee problems and eye and skin conditions are being targeted by managers who intercept referral letters and send them back to GPs rather than allowing them to be seen by the appropriate specialist... Administrators are using referral management schemes to curb hospital admissions...**In north London, all outpatient follow-up appointments are being stopped unless the patient has cancer.** (Emphasis added)

The NHS budgeting system allows so much political influence that some observers conclude:

'The NHS is in crisis, leading to tens of thousands of unnecessary deaths each year...fundamental reform is needed...to address the root cause of the problems of the NHS—that it is a politically controlled state monopoly that is institutionally unresponsive to the needs of patients'[3]

What happens when resource constraints or political considerations enter the healthcare budgetary process and supercede patient need as an allocation parameter? We will examine how the British National Health Service deals with excess demand in terms of <u>waiting lists</u>, <u>equity</u>, <u>technology investment</u> and <u>systemic priorities</u>.

WAITING LISTS

In 1999, over 1,200,000 patients were awaiting inpatient or outpatient treatment in England; Ireland, Wales and Scotland had longer waits.[4] By 2001 this had declined to only about 1,000,000.[5] Of these, over 43,000 had been waiting more than a year[6] The Adam Smith Institute estimates that people currently on NHS waiting lists will collectively wait about one million years longer to receive treatment than doctors deem acceptable.[7]

The Observer reports that delays for colon cancer treatment are so long that 20 percent of these cases considered curable at time of diagnosis are incurable by the time of treatment. Similar results are true of cancer patients. Twenty-five percent of British cardiac patients die while waiting their turn to receive treatment. According to government reports, one in six people on NHS waiting lists for elective surgery are removed without ever being treated. And between 1999 and 2001, 36% of British adult surgery patients had to wait more than 4 months for non-emergency surgery, compared to 5% of American adults.[8]

In response to these long waits, many Britons obtain private health insurance, sometimes supplied as a benefit to key employees. In 2000, some 7 million people (about 11% of the population) had private policies. Most people buy these policies to avoid waiting for medical service. In Britain 'You pay to avoid waiting, or wait to avoid paying.'[9] Some 20% of all surgeries are performed in private hospitals or private beds in NHS hospitals. The private sector specializes in the 'three Hs'—hips, hernias and hemorrhoids, along with some elective surgery, particularly gynecologic and ophthalmologic.[10] Twenty percent of British hip operations are private, as are about half of abortions.[11]

Private coverage, however, is predominately obtained by upper income Britons, primarily in southeastern England near London: some 22% of 'professionals' and 23% of 'employers and managers' had private coverage in 2000, compared to 4% of Scots.[12]

This public / private system allows abuse. Consultants (specialists who control public hospital resource allocations and also work at private hospitals) can control waiting lists. It may be quicker to see the same consultant privately than wait on the NHS list. Or consultants can move preferred patients to the top based on medical or non-medical criterion.

Some specialists have even altered treatment protocols to increase their income. Cardiologists for example may find a partially blocked coronary artery while performing an angiogram. Standard US practice is to perform angioplasty at that time. This reduces the patient risk of two catheter insertions and two anesthetics. It is also more time efficient. But some NHS cardiologists inform the patient, upon waking, of this blockage and then reschedule the angioplasty—with the related lengthy NHS waiting period. The cardiologist may also tell the patient of quicker operating room availability at his private clinic. This is far more lucrative for the cardiologist as the NHS does not regulate private compensation.[13]

The waiting list problem has degenerated to such an extent that **The Observer** reported (October 1, 2006) on people injured in the July 7, 2005 London subway terrorist bombings who had still not been treated at NHS hospitals, even after 15 months. 'We were supposed to be made an NHS priority, but only a handful of specific survivors with extreme injuries have been fast-tracked' claimed Beverli Rhodes.

Rather than continue waiting, Rhodes plans to join the 10 survivors who have so far received medical treatment in Thailand (!). Forty more survivors plan to follow. One survivor, quoted a price of 100,000 British pounds for private treatment in the UK is being charged only 7,000 pounds for the same procedure in Bangkok.

EQUITY

As political factors influence medical resource allocation, areas in Britain with the most political clout get the best medical facilities. The wealthier areas around London have the highest ratio of medical services per capita, and poorer sections of, for example Scotland, have the lowest. This has led the British press to refer to the 'postcode lottery' in which a person's chances of receiving timely, high quality treatment depend on the neighborhood or 'postcode' of residence. [14]

'The Good Hospital Guide', which grades every hospital in Britain on a mortality index, confirmed one indicator of this postcode lottery. Hospitals in wealthy sections of London rated highest on patient mortality scales, while hospitals in the poorest sections rated lowest. London's top 10 hospitals, ranked by mortality, average 52 physicians/100 beds, while the 10 worst average only 31 physicians—a 40% difference! [15]

Britons suffering from renal failure and living in southeastern England have much better access to kidney dialysis centers than others. London has 11 centers within 5 miles of each other and (wealthy and politically important) southeastern England has 16. The rest of the United Kingdom—including all of Scotland, Wales, Northern Ireland and most of England—has only 28 dialysis centers. London and southeastern England have half of the kidney dialysis centers in the UK—but only 26% of the population. [16]

In Scotland, working class Glasgow receives far less than it's fair share of medical services.[17] Glasgow has only 8 cancer specialists per million cancer sufferers, compared to wealthier Edinburgh; with about half of Glasgow's population, Edinburgh has 13. The Beatson Hospital, Scotland's largest cancer treatment center, has 7 specialist radiotherapy machines for 2.7 million people; Edinburgh has 5. (The US averages 6 radiotherapy machines per million people. To match the US average, Glasgow would need 16 machines and Edinburgh 7.) Beatson's underfunding results, according to **Observer** reporter Arnold Kemp, from

> The systematic discrimination against Glasgow from politicians and administrators in Edinburgh that dates from about 1990. The then Scottish Secretary Malcolm Rifkind told me that the substantial public investment in the west of Scotland paid the Tories no political dividends.

Apparently no political payback on election day means little public investment in cancer treatment for Glasgow residents.

TECHNOLOGY INVESTMENT

Britain increased its rate of CT scanners per million people almost 7 fold between 1981 and 2001. This resulted in approximately 25% as many CT scanners per capita in Britain as in the US in 2001.[18]

Number of CT Scanners, US and UK per 1 Million People

	1980	2001
US	6.5	29.4
UK	1.1	7.1

The US National Institutes of Health recommend that every hospital with 200+ beds and a diverse caseload have a CT scanner. The US reached this level in 1985; Britain in 2006.

The British have shown a reluctance to invest in new, expensive technologies until those technologies have proven their worth. This clearly reduces the chance of large investments in unproven technologies, or resources wasted in promising, but ultimately ineffective technologies. The bureaucratic, rigid British healthcare budgeting system resists embracing new technologies.

British NHS bureaucratic budgeters look for a technology financial return on investment. They ask a simple question: is the ROI of CT scanners so much better than X-ray or ultrasound as to justify the huge investment? (They could invest alternatively, for example in expanded dermatology services.) It is difficult to answer this question satisfactorily—and rapidly—for conservative bureaucrats with new technologies. As a result the British have severely lagged American medical breakthroughs, and British treatment protocols sometimes seem almost archaic to American physicians.

We can note three effects on the National Health Service of British failure to invest in CT technologies in the 1980s.

First, the lack of CT scanners reduced perceived demand for information generated by this technology. With weak demand, the British invested fewer resources in training radiologists. As a result, even after the British began budgeting for more scanners, they faced the human resource constraint of an insufficiently trained radiology community. Films were often read by (less well trained) radiographers.

Second, the lack of scanners and trained radiologists meant that diagnosticians were unable to specialize in different organs. The US developed radiology specializations in the mid-1980s: chest radiologists, GI radiologists, neuroradiologists, etc. The British, by contrast, either relied on a 'radiology generalists' or on older, less sophisticated diagnostic tools such as X-rays and ultra-sound until recently.

Third, waits for CT diagnosis extended to almost unbelievable periods. British reports of waiting periods for non-life threatening (though potentially very painful) conditions such as lumbar back or knee problems extended to 10—24 months.

New technology diffusion in Britain is slower than in America. We spend more on technology, often choosing to invest when the British would watch, wait and consider the ROI versus other investment options more carefully. Clearly the Americans sometimes get it wrong and invest unwisely.

But a more fundamental question underlies this technology discussion. How would American consumers react if our medical system adopted the British 'go slow' approach to new technologies? Would Americans with painful joints or suspected cancers accept that 'we can't offer you the latest diagnostic technology because we're unsure it's ROI, so we'll use an older, less dynamic, less clear, less certain diagnostic tool'?

I think that Americans always want the best, the latest, the clearest, the most robust technology available when their health is at stake. More on this later.

SYSTEMIC PRIORITIES

The British have made a fundamental healthcare finance choice that differs from Americas. The British have decided that, due to severe financial constraints, they will accept a 'modified utilitarian' (my term) approach to healthcare investment.

We will define 'modified utilitarian' in two ways. **First,** in the classic 'greatest good for the greatest number' without spending too much on healthcare. The British believe that resources are finite, and that they must protect the financial strength of British economic society by investing only an 'appropriate' amount in healthcare. This may cause some sick or elderly to receive sub-optimal treatment—apparently an acceptable price to pay for economic stability. Most people get adequate medical care. The overriding public investment goal is the financial stability of British society.

This philosophy resonates in Gordon Brown's 2005 'Chancellor of the Exchequer's Budget Statement' (Brown became Prime Minister in 2007): [19]

- 'My Budget choice is to lock in stability and never put it at risk'
- 'Our first fiscal rule is to balance the current budget'
- 'I firmly believe that a shared British national purpose (is)... that we never...take risks with stability'
- 'Stability the foundation'

This contradicts the American medical approach which we can summarize as 'do everything possible for the individual' even if this includes paying the highest healthcare prices in the world (by a large margin). American medical malpractice lawyers, for example, make their livings by showing where providers failed to do everything possible for the individual. American society is far more individual-centric than Britain.

Our second definition of 'modified utilitarian' somewhat contradicts the first. We can state this as 'Exceptions to rule #1 exist when high profile or highly publicized medical failures may have significant negative effects on the Government.' The British try to invest in medical procedures that limit the number of publicly seen sick children or other situations that might make the Government look badly. By contrast, the British limit investments to sick elderly who likely will not appear in newspapers.

We can demonstrate this 'modified utilitarianism' by contrasting the British healthcare investment in kidney dialysis and hemophelia.[20]

BRITISH KIDNEY DISEASE TREATMENT

Kidney failure allows toxins to accumulate in the body. Untreated, kidney failure can lead to death. There are two main types of treatment: dialysis and transplant. And there are two main types of dialysis: hemodialysis and peritoneal dialysis.

In hemodialysis, the patient's blood flows via a catheter into a blood-cleansing machine. Treatment takes several hours, several times per week in a dialysis center. Hemodialysis has good treatment success rates. This increases demand for machines and dialysis centers as people live longer and thus need their machines longer. In 2005, British hemodialysis costs averaged about $45,000 per patient per year.[21]

Peritoneal dialysis can be home based. It is much cheaper. Here a special solution is inserted into the abdominal cavity via a plastic tube. Waste products move into the solution by osmosis and then exit the body. The fluid is periodically drained and replaced. This requires a very low NHS investment—typically just a monthly solution refill and an occasional check-in from an NHS visiting nurse. However, peritoneal dialysis can put significant time and skill demands on the patient's family. If these are inappropriately managed the patient's health may suffer.

Kidney transplants are the most complex of options. Transplants require a donor, a highly skilled medical operating staff, hospital resources and a sufficiently ill patient to warrant the medical risks. One constraint on transplants: number of available donors. (British law until recently imposed restrictions on kidney donations from strangers.) British transplant rates have sometimes been higher than US rates. One suspected reason: the inadequacy of home supports for peritoneal dialysis, which results in unsuccessful treatment and need for life saving transplant surgery.

Dialysis centers operate on fixed annual budgets without regard to patient demand. This provides financial incentives for nephrologists to prescribe peritoneal (home) dialysis or transplant.

Dialysis and Transplant Rates, US and UK 1980 and 2002

1980 - # procedures per million population

	US	UK	
Hemodialysis	190	60	
Peritoneal Dialysis	3	9	(Peritoneal is 13% of UK dialysis total
Transplant	42	56	but only 1.5% of US total.)
Total	**249**	**128**	(UK does 51% of US total)

2002 - # procedures per million population

	US	UK	
Hemodialysis	978	244	
Peritoneal Dialysis	86	92	(Peritoneal is 27% of UK dialysis total
Transplant	424	289	but only 8% of US total.)
Total	**1496**	**625**	(UK does 42% of US total)

In the 1980s, British treated patients up to age 44 at about the same rate as other western European countries, but treated few over 50 and almost none over 55. Interestingly, the British believed that they provided optimal care at this time. They believed that over-55's were 'a bit crumbly' and inappropriate for care. They also rejected diabetics or people with co-morbidities. The British attitude can be summarized by this nephrologist, making a statement to a child of a 65 year old suffering from renal failure in the 1980s:

> 'I would say that your mother's kidneys are failing and there is little anybody can do about it because of her age and general physical state, and that would be my suggestion or advice that we spare her any further investigation, and further painful procedure, and we would just make her as comfortable as we can for what remains of her life.'

This nephrologist apparently believes that societal resources can best be spent elsewhere; that the potential longevity or life quality gains for this 65-year-old are insufficient to justify the medical cost. The patient's family, unlike typical Americans, accepted the physicians recommendations without demanding a second opinion or access to another facility. The NHS suffered in the 1980s from very tight budgets and scare financial resources. This nephrologist practiced the British modified utilitarian philosophy.

By 2002, NHS funding levels increased and nearly 50% of new British dialysis patients were over 65 years old. Apparently, the elderly respond better to kidney treatment when funding becomes available!

Renal failure patients suffer privately. They may appear weak but generally otherwise look normal. Theirs is not a disease that attracts widespread public displays of interest, protest or comment. They receive treatment behind closed doors. When their illness becomes acute they pass away fairly quickly without big public displays.

This is not the case for hemophilia.

BRITISH TREATMENT OF HEMOPHELIA

Hemophilia is a bleeding disease usually diagnosed in children, that if untreated leads to suffering, disability and death. However, modern treatment—blood transfusion based—can allow hemophiliacs to have close to normal lives and life expectancies.

In the early 1980s when Britain operated the National Health Service under very severe financial constraints, the average annual treatment cost per hemophiliac was about $6,000. This has grown to over $100,000 post-2000.

The total 2001 population of hemophiliacs in Britain was only about 6300. Of these, about 2300 were deemed 'severe' cases, which represented about 90% of the total approximately $290 million total hemophilia treatment costs...less than 3/10 of 1% of the total NHS budget.

The British treat almost all hemophiliacs according to need, apparently without regard to the severe budgetary constraints faced by renal sufferers.[22] There seem three reasons for this.

First, the relatively small number of hemophiliacs in the 1970s and 1980s, combined with the relatively low annual treatment costs made treatment of the entire hemophiliac population inexpensive.

Budget decision-makers **second,** seem to have decided in the 1970s and 1980s to treat this group fully, rather than allow the small hemophiliac population to suffer painfully and visibly. This budgetary decision seems to represent a public relations decision—a desire to avoid an adverse public reaction to letting young people suffer visibly. (The British hemophiliac population is relatively vocal, as evidenced by their loud public outcry over tainted blood used in transfusions in the early 2000s.) [23]

Third, changing the NHS policy, institutionalized over many years, became more difficult than offering hemophiliacs only partial treatment, just as Michels would have predicted.

In 2005, some 6,000 patients were still on kidney treatment waiting lists (at $45,000 treatment costs/capita or less) while all 6300 hemophiliacs received appropriate treatment (at $100,000 treatment costs/capita or more).[25]

VALUES

Our analysis of the British NHS as a single payer system example leads to one clear conclusion: healthcare cost control comes from restricting healthcare services. The British restrictions include:

- number of hospital employees, by the budgetary process,
- number of physicians, by budgets, medical school acceptance policies and physician licensing policies,

- number of procedures, by annual budgets
- number of specialist visits, by GP referral power and hospital management procedures,
- number of medical tests, by waiting lists
- technology investment, by budgets

The British public and medical establishment, by-and-large, accept these restrictions even while complaining about the NHS. Britons seem to accept the modified utilitarian philosophy that economic conservatism and stability are more important than some excessive, potentially life-saving medical expenditures. As a British physician summarized attitudes of his colleagues:

> If physicians over here had infinite resources, they would treat person-for-person less people than...in the US...a different attitude to end stage renal failure...I think (US dialysis rates are) just an example of modern interventional technology being misused...I'd put more resources into end of life management, skilled palliative care facilities, proper care for the dying...I'd recognize end stage renal failure as a legitimate cause of death that should be managed and not complicated by an uncritical application of dialysis.[26]

Americans, we have argued, demand more healthcare options. We have voted with our pocketbooks since the 1990s for fewer managed care restrictions, easier referrals and wider provider access. Though we often complain about health insurance prices, we are generally loath to trade-off lower cost plans for tighter carrier restrictions as evidenced by the growth of PPO and POS health insurance plans.

Would Americans embrace an NHS type single payer system even if it would cut our healthcare expenditures in half? I suspect not for Americans have a different value structure than Britons. I suspect that Americans, when faced with public waiting lists, healthcare inequality and slow embrace of new technologies would turn to the private sector for help. We have demonstrated over the past 50 years that choice is our primary criterion in healthcare consumption: we want to choose our own doctor, hospital and method of treatment, and not have that choice imposed by the government or an insurance carrier. And we want our healthcare treatments now, on our timetable, not next year, on the governments'.

I suspect that imposition of a tightly controlled, budget-constrained single payer system like the NHS in American would, almost by definition, stimulate the private sector to offer health insurance policies. I do not believe that American healthcare consumers would accept the modified utilitarian approach of Britain. We are too habituated to demand that we each individually receive all the treatment available, almost regardless the price.

Our demands for access, choice and excessive care would doom an NHS type, cost-conscious single payer system. Such a system would, almost by definition, become two systems: one funded publicly and the other privately, perhaps based on employment or employer contributions. Employers who want to attract and retain the best employees would offer the most attractive health insurance plans. Top employees would seek these employee benefits. And we would recreate a system much like our current one.

The basic problem Americans have with the British NHS is the restrictions: the reason the NHS works economically is exactly the reason most Americans would not like it. As such, it is an inappropriate solution to America's healthcare problem.

CHAPTER 9
Case Study: Medicare

Medicare is a single payer system that provides health coverage to elderly Americans.

The Physicians for a National Health Plan hold Medicare as the single payer healthcare model. Medicare insures about 42 million elderly or disabled Americans. Its overhead runs under 2% of total program cost. It's in place, has plenty of experience and could—presumably fairly easily—expand to cover everyone. Why not?

First, Medicare hemorrhages money.[1] Expenditures more than tripled from $109 billion in 1990 to $336 billion in 2005.[2] Between 2004 and 2005, Medicare expenditures grew by $35 billion or 11%—more than 3 times the 3.4% Consumer Price Index—while enrollment grew by a slim 1.4%.[3]

Since its inception, Medicare spending has grown more than 14 times the rate of inflation. In a decade or so according to some estimates, spending will top half a trillion dollars annually and consume nearly a fourth of the Federal budget.[4]

There are few, in any incentives to control medical treatment costs prudently. Providers, especially in high retiree-states like Florida, often live off of Medicare. And it is well documented that Medicare beneficiaries will undertake treatment as long as the value of that care is more than the copayment for which they are responsible.[5]

Politicians have no incentives to tackle Medicare funding and cost control problems, for any change that leaves the elderly worse off will lead to ballot box reprisals from a large, vocal and politically active segment of society. And providers have little incentive to controls costs through, for example, cheaper treatment alternatives, for their self interest runs counter...a classic case of moral hazard.

Even beyond moral hazard problems, outright Medicare fraud runs billions annually. Dara Corrigan, Acting Principal Deputy Inspector

General, testified to the House Budget Committee on July 9, 2003 that 'improper payments under Medicare's fee-for-service system totaled an estimated $13.3 billion during 2002.'

The US General Accounting Offices claims that there has been only limited progress in bringing fiscal discipline to Medicare.[6] 'It is astonishing' according to Arnold Millstein, a medical quality expert and Medicare advisory board member, 'We are medically impoverishing increasing numbers of Americans in part because of our inattention to eliminating waste.' Medicare spends just 15/100ths of 1% of funding to oversee and improve patient care [7] and to assure provider compliance with its 100,000+ pages of regulations.

Medicare has been called a 'multi-trillion-dollar mistake that encapsulates all that is wrong with the modern social welfare state...[it] encourages all takers to consume as much medical care as possible— but always at the expense of others.'[8] Credible commentators claim it's a 'dysfunctional healthcare system'[9] with a 'stupid reimbursement structure.'[10] Total 1990 Medicare hospital expenditures were more than 6 times higher than originally forecast in 1965, just 25 years before.

Second, Medicare exhibits little quality control. Dartmouth Medical School researchers estimate that 20% of Medicare expenditures go to procedures that provide no benefit in terms of longevity or improved quality of life and $1 of every $3 is wasted on unnecessary or inappropriate care. [11]

How can this be? We'll look at Medicare problems from 3 vantage points: consumer demand, quality control, and government meddling.

Consumer demand. Average Medicare spending on beneficiaries in Miami during their last 6 months of life was about double the Medicare spending on patients in Minneapolis during their last 6 months, according to a study by Dartmouth's Jonathan Skinner and John Wennberg [12]. Average ICU days were nearly 4 times higher in Miami. Average Miami Medicare patients had 440% more specialist visits during their last 6 months that did Medicare patients in Minneapolis.

These Medicare patients in their last 6 months of life were generally quite ill. There is no evidence that the spending differences were due to underlying variations in health levels across the regions. Rather they are linked to the various services available and demanded by consumers—

specialist visits, diagnostic tests, home health services and minor procedures. 'There is just no evidence that doing more helps' according to Dartmouth's Fisher. 'At best you do the same, and in some cases you actually do worse' [13] due to infections, errors, patient fatigue, etc.

In Minneapolis, home health services are 39% of the national average, while in Miami they are 60% above average, meaning their ratio is roughly 4 to 1. By contrast, the inpatient service ratio is only 1.5 to 1, suggesting that services with the greatest discretionary (and profitability) component—home health and laboratory services—are the ones most sensitive to geographic location.

'There appears to be little correlation between the intensity of care near the end of life and mortality rates, whether intensity is measured by spending, days in the hospital, or ICU days near the end of life,' according to the study.

What explains these cost differences? After all, Medicare is a federal program with national standards and provider reimbursement rates, modified slightly for cost of living variations geographically. The authors suggest that

> 'one reason could be the sheer amount of resources in Miami, more hospital beds per thousand (Roemer's Law??) and more specialists (46% more in Miami). Another explanation could be the much higher ratio of for-profit hospital beds in Miami, 56 percent versus 2 percent in Minneapolis...(still another) could in the structure of physician groups rather than hospitals. The interaction between patient demand and physician behavior is also important in understanding the practice of medicine in Miami...elderly patients come to expect numerous referrals as the norm, and would suspect physicians who do not refer them to other physicians.'

Wennberg gives an interesting explanation of this process.[14] There is no clear rulebook for dealing with chronically ill patients. When should an elderly cancer patient who also suffers from congestive heart disease be admitted to hospital either for treatment or observation? How ill must a patient be for a physician to prescribe home health care? How often should a patient suffering from congestive heart failure be seen by a cardiologist—every 2 months? Every 3 months? Every 4 months? Wennberg suggests that the physician 'will sort it out based on how sick an individual patient is and <u>how many openings her has in his schedule.</u> Specialists tend to fill their appointment books to capacity' (italics my own) making it easy to see how increasing the supply of cardiologists would mean patients will see their physicians more often.

Another factor: Medicare payment practices. Medicare sometimes contracts directly with providers and pays fee-for-service. Other times Medicare contracts with an HMO and pays a flat fee/member. Medicare calculates that fee, in part, on fee-for-service costs per patient in that region.

The result: HMOs located where patients use more services receive higher payments/member than HMOs in lower cost regions. WellCare, a Miami HMO, received $11,823 per Medicare member in 2003; HealthPartners in Minneapolis received $7,851.

Yet HealthPartners outperformed WellCare on 13 of 14 Medicare quality measures such as percent of enrollees getting flu shots or colorectal exams.[15] Medicare does not tie payments to quality. So over the average lifetime of a Medicare patient, low quality Miami Medicare beneficiaries receive about a $50,000 subsidy from high quality Minneapolis Medicare recipients.

Patients are also complicit in this Miami Medicare extravaganza.[16] Doctor visits

'have become a social activity...Many patients have 8, 10 or 12 specialists and visit one or more of them most days of the week. They bring their spouses and plan their days around their appointments, going out to eat or shopping while they are in the area. They know what they want; they choose specialists for every body part. And every visit, every procedure is covered by Medicare...Boca Raton, researchers agree, is a case study of what happens when people are given free rein to have all the medical care they could imagine.'

How do patients find appropriate specialists? Leon Bloomberg, age 83 tells us: 'You get recommendations at the clubhouse, at the swimming pool. You go to a restaurant here and 9 out of 10 times, before the meal is over, you hear people talking about a doctor.' The traditional Medicare fee-for-service system acts like a PPO, with no Primary Care referrals needed. Apparently Miami residents think clubhouse friends and swimming pool companions have equal diagnostic and referral credibility to technically trained primary care physicians.

Providers claim excessive patient demand—patients want lots of tests and specialists, they refer themselves to specialists and they ask for and get far more medical attention than many doctors think is reasonable or advisable. The Medicare card is 'like a gold card that lets you go to any doctor you want' claims Dr. Robert Colton, a Boca Raton internist. 'I see it every day.'

But Dr. Colton sounds a cautionary note, worrying that Primary Care Physicians cannot perform their gate-keeping function properly. 'When there's no control on utilization, (physicians take) the path of least resistance. If a patient says 'My shoulder hurts, I want an MRI, I want to see a shoulder specialist,' the path of least resistance is to send them off. You have nothing to gain by refusing.'

(One potential underlying reason. Medicare, like all of US healthcare, has little outcome data. Patients do not know which hospitals, PCPs, diagnosticians or specialists generate the best patient outcomes. As a result patients want more tests and more procedures, figuring that the last specialist might have missed something. See below for a discussion of Medicare's poor quality controls.)

'The doctors are raping Medicare' claims Louis Ziegler, a retired manufacturer living in nearby Delray Beach. He recalled doctor's visit for a chronic finger problem and requested a cortisone shot. But he got much more. 'I had diathermy. I had ultrasound. I had a paraffin massage. I had $600 worth of Medicare treatments to get my lousy $35 shot of cortisone.'

In other words, moral hazard rules in Miami. Patients demand service, providers bill and Medicare pays—about double per capita compared to Minneapolis for approximately the same epidemiological population, with no obvious longevity or life quality improvements. Medicare is unable to control itself; Miami Medicare subscribers self-diagnose and self-refer, apparently at whim. Everyone, it seems, takes advantage of the fact that 'Medicare pays.'

Unfortunately, the Miami—Minneapolis price and quality differentials are but examples of the wider problem. In another study, the Dartmouth researchers divided the US into 10 deciles, based on Medicare payment rates. (At the extreme, payments per Medicare beneficiary range from $3,053 in Iowa to $10,373 in DC.)[17] After studying patient hospital utilization, costs and outcomes, they concluded 'Residents of high-spending regions received 60 percent more care but did not have lower mortality rates, better functional status or higher satisfaction.' More money simply resulted in more physician visits, specialist consultations, tests and greater use of hospital and intensive care facilities,[18] with no better and sometimes slightly worse outcomes.[19]

Quality Controls. Medicare controls quality through a complex system of accreditation and oversight contractors.[20] Medicare spends millions on quality controls annually:

1. Over $100 million for hospital accreditation;
2. Over $250 million to state regulators to investigate complaints and inspect healthcare facilities;
3. Nearly $300 annually to private groups in each state called Quality Improvement Organizations that work closely with hospitals to improve care.

The 1965 Medicare legislation contained language that delegated hospital quality evaluation to the **Joint Commission on the Accreditation of Healthcare Organizations**. This nonprofit currently receives over $100 million annually to accredit Medicare providers. Interestingly, its mission is to help hospitals and other facilities meet Medicare standards, not to relegate or punish them; it has no sanctioning powers. It also owns **Joint Commission Resources,** a for-profit subsidiary that advises hospitals how to pass accreditation reviews. About 99% of the hospitals reviewed by the Joint Commission win accreditation. Joint Commission Resources, which bills hospitals for its advice, paid it's parent over $10 million between 2000—2003 in management fees.

Some state regulators claim that the Joint Commission and similar groups are too closely aligned with the health facilities they review. Nelson Sabatini, Maryland's health commissioner for example, called this system 'a fraud' with poor oversight. 'The fundamental structure of the joint commission doesn't make sense. It's one big built-in conflict, and the fact that Medicare allows it is appalling.' Medicare spot-checks the Joint Commission's work: in 2003 it reviewed 1% of all hospital accreditation surveys.

But Medicare officials say they are required by law to use the joint commission's congressionally mandated accreditation system, virtually whatever the quality, due to 1965 legislation. The Medicare statue explicitly specifies that any provider who meets the entry requirements is entitled to participate in Medicare and that patients are free to choose any provider who will have them, regardless of quality. [21] Indeed, the first two sentences of the original Medicare statute state:

> Nothing in this title shall be construed to authorize any Federal officer or employee to exercise any supervision or control over the practice of medicine or the manner in which medical services are provided, or over the selection, tenure, or compensation of any officer or employee of any institution, agency, or person providing health services; or to exercise any supervision or control over the administration or operation of any such institution, agency, or person. Any individual entitled to insurance benefits under this title may obtain health services from any institution, agency, or person qualified to participate under this title if such institution, agency, or person undertakes to provide him with services.[22]

See next section on Government Meddling for more.

Fifty-three **Quality Improvement Organizations** (QIOs) receive almost $300 million annually from Medicare to measure quality, work with hospitals and doctors to improve care and investigate patient complaints. By law, QIOs operate in secrecy with little oversight or accountability and generally prefer to cooperate with hospitals, rather than sanction them. 'One of the problems with QIOs is that they are reluctant to do anything that ruins their relationships with providers' according to Robert A. Berenson, a Medicare official in the Clinton administration.

How well do QIOs work? In 2003 and 2004, they received a total of about 3,100 patient complaints—about 1 for every 14,000 Medicare beneficiaries. They sanctioned about 1 doctor each year in the early 2000s. QIO executives claim they are hamstrung by Medicare's decades-old rules that place a premium on secrecy. They are even prohibited from publicly naming the hospitals they work with unless the facilities agree. (Few do.)

Medicare officials audit QIOs but declined a Washington Post request for audit copies, and did not respond to Freedom of Information requests for that information during the 17 months prior to the Post writing its Medicare analysis in 2005.

State regulators also receive Medicare money to monitor hospital quality, but again often to little effect. A brief case study of Palm Beach Gardens Medical Center, a 204 bed hospital in Florida illustrates the problems.

During the 1990s, Palm Beach Gardens performed over 1,000 open heart procedures annually. State regulators received complaints about the high rate of patient infections in 1999 but dismissed them. Public lawsuits forced the state to reconsider in 2002.

During a 3-day inspection, the state reviewed records of 24 heart patients and found that 13—that's 54%!—developed serious infections after their surgical procedures, some requiring major, re-constructive surgery. (I do not know if this was a random survey. Note however that Medicare pays for the second operation also—even if performed at Palm Beach Gardens—creating a potential provider conflict of interest regarding infection reduction.) The state notified Medicare, which subsequently informed the hospital that it was 'out of compliance' with Medicare requirements and conditions posed an 'immediate jeopardy to patient's health and safety.' Medicare threatened to remove Palm Beach Garden from its program.

Medicare never delivered on this threat. The hospital filed a 'plan of correction,' Medicare backed-off its threat and did nothing. Medicare rarely expels hospitals from its program, even the dangerous ones.

State regulators fined the hospital $323,800, but quickly reduced this to $95,000 to avoid a lengthy process; the Hospital has significant political influence, and did not acknowledge any wrongdoing.

After suffering a short-term drop-off in business, Palm Beach Gardens is once again busy. It touts its heart program as among the nation's best. We have no information on results of its 'plan of correction' because neither Medicare nor the State of Florida (nor any other credible organization) releases audited outcome data.

But Miami Medicare costs are still among the highest in the country—regardless of the results.

Government Meddling. Unlike the British and Canadians, where tradition and regulation keeps the government from micromanaging healthcare, the US Congress seems comfortable meddling with Medicare.

This is due in part to Medicare's origins and structure. When created in 1965, the government needed support from providers and provider organizations. They consequently agreed on an open-ended, fee-for-service payment system that could only be changed by act of Congress. As Medicare prices rose (along with raising fears about tax hikes to pay for entitlements), Congress changed from a 'usual and customary' to Prospective Payment System based on Diagnostic Related Groups for hospitals (1983) and physicians (1992).

These administrative pricing mechanisms allow providers to use their political clout to lobby for special treatment. Why is this? According to former CMS administrator Bruce Vladeck 'Medicare cannot deliver services to its beneficiaries without providers and because providers are major sources of campaign contributions in every congressional district.' [23] Medicare compensates providers for their medical inputs (procedures performed or time spent with patients) rather than on their outcomes (hospitals with higher post-operative infection rates, for example, getting paid less), with predictable results. [24]

We'll explore how this works with the Congressionally mandated End-Stage Renal Disease program. [25]

In 1973 Congress passed the ESRDP to provide federal support for most patients with end-stage renal disease. Prior to this, the new technology of kidney dialysis was too expensive for most people even with medical insurance. In 1965, for example fewer than 150 people were dialyzed nationally even though tens of thousands were medically qualified.

Time Magazine claimed that with this program 'for the first time, the Government will accept responsibility for a group of patients regardless of age, occupation or financial status' [26] and the program looked benevolent and popular.

But Congress decided not only to cover costs, but also to stipulate protocols, standards, national reimbursement rates, frequency of dialysis, approved types of testing, etc. This made Congress both the financier and medical decision-maker. Neither patients nor providers could deviate from the Congressional cookbook formula. The only patient choice: treatment site.

Currently dialysis costs about $65,000 per person per year. If patients have private insurance, the carrier pays for 33 months of treatment and then Medicare pays, regardless of patient age. Medicare accounts for about 90% of ESRDP payments and covers about 300,000 patients.

Does this program work well? While expenditures more than tripled from $5.1 billion in 1991 to $18.4 billion in 2004, the death rates in the first year of dialysis for end-stage renal disease patients remained about the same from 1993—2004, as did hospital admissions and lengths of stay.[27] This is much as one would expect, since all treatment variables were mandated, bureaucratically codified and resistant to change regardless of medical technology improvements. It's also a testament to Robert Michels observation about the power of administrators to end reform movements by stifling innovation.

'All too many patients did not receive the preventive care that could slow the progression of their diseases' according to Harvard's Regina Herzlinger, for the Congressionally approved treatment did not pay for prevention, only cookie-cutter treatment. 'Because providers must follow Congress's recipe, kidney disease victims…can die prematurely, injured by the shortage of the testing and health promoting services they need and the excessive drugs they received,' for the Congressionally mandated treatment consisted of drug therapy for all patients.'[28]

In other words, we likely pay too much for the wrong kind of care. ESRDP treatment pricing does not include prevention, testing or wellness activities that could have mitigated progression of the other diseases that frequently accompany kidney disease. Remember Manhattan's Beth Israel Hospital diabetes control program failure? Diabetes is a key cause of kidney failure.

Who benefits from ESRDP? According to Herzlinger, 'the businesspeople who understood the care and feeding of our Congress earned millions.'[29]

DaVita is a publicly traded company that owns a quarter of all dialysis centers in the US; its CEO earned over $25 million in 2005. Amgen is the biotechnology firm that manufactures epoetin, the drug primarily used for people on dialysis. Its stock price grew more than 50% annually in the 1990s and it earned nearly $4 billion in 2005 profits. Its CEO earned nearly $20 million in 2005, on top of nearly $50 million in options

Amgen spent $5.7 million on lobbying in 2005.[30] DaVita spent about $1 million on federal lobbying during the first half of 2006. The Los Angeles Times says this million led to an annual $100 million increase in Medicare payments to dialysis providers.[31]

In addition, Congress, through Medicare authorizations, set the target range for hematocrit—a measure of oxygen-carrying red blood cells that is directly impacted by epo. Hematocrit target levels were raised over time from 30% to 33% and finally to 36% in 2006. According to Harvard's Herzlinger, 'one powerful senator personally requested that the Medicare administrators increase the upper end level of the hematocrit... he chaired the subcommittee that supervises the budget for Medicare.'[32] This increased spending on epo by about $500 million annually, for a 3% increase in hematocrit requires up to a 50% increase in epo dosage.[33]

Unfortunately, 'patients assigned to higher hematocrit target levels do not show discernable improvements in survival, hospitalization or cardiac outcomes. In fact, they could be prone to adverse cardiovascular events that include heart attacks and strokes.'[34]

Congress also mandated that dialysis treatment in hospitals receive $4 more than in stand alone clinics, per treatment, due to the higher hospital cost structure. But Medicare notes that treatments and outcomes are the same in hospitals and clinics. This amounts to a taxpayer subsidy for hospital inefficiency and is, perhaps, related to the $17 million that hospitals and related organizations spent on lobbying and contributions in 2004.[35]

As a result of Congressional meddling and program micro-management: [36]

- 'In most chains and hospital-based centers, fewer than half the patients had good results for diabetes or the important tests for the heart diseases that typically accompany diabetes, and two-thirds had excessive levels of protein in their urine, a dangerous sign of the lack of efficacy of the dialysis.'
- Although many kidney dialysis patients are also diabetic, 'less than half of these very sick patients received comprehensive diabetic monitoring in 2004 or flu vaccine, despite their appearance in the dialysis centers at least three times each week.'
- Use of Epo increased. Congress favored it in the cost-plus payment formula it chose for drugs, so gave the manufacturer

a virtual monopoly by granting it a special designation 'orphan drug'. This prohibits similar drugs from going through the government clearance process for 7 years and grants a 50% tax credit on clinical trials among other advantages.

- Medicare codification, mandates, orphan drug designations and micromanagement of ESRDP inhibited alternative treatments from being developed.

The government has been intimately involved in Medicare operations since its inception in 1965. Robert Ball, Social Security commissioner under Presidents Kennedy, Johnson and Nixon, claimed Medicare was designed to face the least possible political opposition. It gave something to everyone—the American Medical Association, hospitals, patients and politicians to get the program passed by Congress and accepted by providers. [37]

Congress began micromanaging Medicare at inception by setting minimum care standards for hospitals, called 'conditions of participation'. Interestingly, those standards were initially credited with improving the quality of care, circa 1965. Over time, however, they have lagged behind medical improvements, and attempts to update them have often failed due to politics or bureaucracy [38]—just as Robert Michels predicted.

This does not occur as much in Canada or Britain where politicians generally stop meddling once funding is set. Americans have established a government meddling tradition with Medicare—naming the accreditation organizations, specifying hematocrit levels, differentiating payments by provider type—under political pressure and to the detriment of the programs evolution.

How does this affect Medicare's financial situation? Is it financially solvent and thus a good model for single payer healthcare in America?

Every year the Medicare Board of Trustees reports to Congress on the state of Medicare's financial health. The 2006 Report said that Medicare's Hospital Insurance Trust Fund is projected to be exhausted in 2018—2 **years earlier than had been forecast just the year before!** [39]

The 2007 Report was also dire, claiming:

- 'The financial condition of the…Medicare program remains problematic';
- Compared to Social Security, 'Medicare's financial status is even worse';

- The Hospital Insurance Trust Fund 'again fails our test of short-range financial adequacy...and fail(s) our long-range test of close actuarial balance by a wide margin'; and
- Issued a 'Medicare funding warning.'[40]

What is Medicare's underlying actuarial situation? Medicare was designed in 1960s when we had about 4.5 working employees paying into the system for each beneficiary taking money out of the system. It was originally designed as a 'pay-as-you-go' system—designed to receive tax money annually from employee-based taxes but not fully capitalized based on expected payout rates.

That was not an unreasonable financing structure given the political realities of the 1960s and anticipated future systemic demands.

Today, however, there are only about 4 workers paying in for each beneficiary taking out, and each beneficiary is taking out far more than anticipated in 1965. According to Medicare's trustees, by 2030 there will be only 2.4 payers vs. beneficiary, making 'pay as you go' financially perilous even if payout rates / beneficiary buck their historical trend and do not increase. But remember the history: lifetime geriatric spending has increased 11 fold, inflation adjusted, for 65+ year olds for from 1960 to 2000.

(I once presented this information to a class that included a former banker. I asked if he would lend to a client who presented like Medicare. His shocked response: 'Absolutely not!')

Continued Medicare financial viability requires one of four strategies. **First**, we could cut Medicare benefits—probably currently politically impossible. **Second**, we could increase taxes to support the current benefit levels—again politically quite unattractive.

Third, we could increase private insurance subsidies to Medicare recipients. Medicare underpaid hospitals by $15.5 billion in 2004 according to data presented by the American Hospital Association.[41] Underpayment is the difference between the actual costs incurred by hospitals for treating Medicare patients and the reimbursement received from Medicare. This difference is covered by private sector insurance and grows annually.

How much does each private insurance policy currently subsidize Medicare? Blue Shield of California estimates that it could reduce premiums by almost 10% if all government programs paid the same amount as the private sector.[42] The Medicare subsidy alone was almost $650 from each 2004 California private family health insurance policy.[43] As Medicare's underpayments grow—due to hospital costs increasing faster than payroll taxes—so does this subsidy. Probably not a good long term solution.

Fourth, we could capitalize Medicare. This means we could deposit into Medicare's trust fund the amount of money needed for future liabilities, and then invest that money to allow for growth in beneficiaries' medical expenses. This would alleviate the need to reduce benefits or raise taxes.

The Centers for Medicare and Medicaid Services estimate the present value of Medicare's unfunded liabilities at $68 trillion.[44] So we could fully capitalize Medicare by depositing $68 trillion in its trust fund.

Unfortunately, the current US GDP is only $12 trillion—about 1/5 the amount needed to capitalize Medicare. Fully capitalizing Medicare would take the entire output of the US economy for about 5 years. (Note: this is not just the value of US government spending; it is the value of all public and private economic activity.)

We could, of course, ask for international help. The current Gross World Product, estimated by the World Bank, is about $41 trillion. So if the world decided to help us out, we could fully capitalize Medicare by taking the entire value of all goods and services produced by every inhabitant of the globe for a year and a half. In other words, *it would take all 4 billion world inhabitants working exclusively on this for a year and a half to solve the healthcare financing problem of 42 million elderly Americans.*

We could, of course, use a combination of benefit reductions, tax increases, cost shifting and/or capitalization to rescue Medicare. I cannot speculate on what that package might look like.

Perhaps this is what Professors Richmond and Fein meant by 'The Healthcare Mess'.

***

How does Medicare rate on the 6 healthcare system problems discussed in Chapter 4?

1. **High number of uninsured:** Medicare is excellent at insuring everyone who qualifies. This is its major success.

2. **The Medical Arms Race:** Medicare is dreadful at controlling hospital technology expenditures and contributes to—rather than mitigates against—unnecessary technology spending.

3. **Moral hazard:** Medicare is perhaps the quintessential force behind unnecessary medical spending. It allows beneficiaries virtually unfettered access to virtually any provider and wastes up to 30% of its money.

4. **Chronic disease care and prevention:** Medicare gets consistently low marks for its preventive and chronic disease control programs. Medicare pays by DRG for procedures, not for prevention.

5. **Uneven treatment quality nationwide:** Medicare pays twice as much for beneficiaries in Miami than in Minneapolis. There is very little uniformity of cost/beneficiary nationally, due partially to the lack of moral hazard control and partially to the lack of outcome data.

6. **Quality and safety investments:** Medicare has almost no quality controls or enforcement mechanisms. It sanctions about 1 physician annually and almost never cancels a hospital contract.

Medicare is not a good national single payer healthcare system model. It wastes money, cannot control itself and is going broke. It fails to fund preventive or chronic disease treatment programs adequately, but overpays for procedures that, according to Dartmouth researchers, do 'nothing for longevity, nothing for patient satisfaction and nothing for better access to care'.[45] And it certainly costs a lot.

Medicare reflects the key healthcare value of most Americans—wide choice among providers with virtually unfettered access. Absent almost any quality controls, cost controls or published outcome data, Medicare has turned itself into an ATM machine for the elderly: it simply pays.

That is why the average American, 65+ years old, now consumes an inflation adjusted $147,000 during their remaining lifetime, up from an inflation adjusted $11,500 in 1960…and why this 11 fold increase has resulted in life expectancy gains of just 1.7 years.[46]

What a mess! Surely there's a better single payer example available.

CHAPTER 10
US Veterans Administration Healthcare System

The VHA is a single payer system that provides health coverage to veterans.

The US Veterans Administration is an American single payer system that differs greatly from Medicare. Many see the Veterans Healthcare Administration (VHA) system as the best single payer model currently available.[1]

The VHA provides outstanding patient care:

- The New England Journal of Medicine published a 2003 study that used 11 quality measures to compare fee-for-service Medicare with VHA health facilities. The VHA was 'significantly better' on all 11 measures;[2]
- The Annals of Internal Medicine published similar results on a 2004 study that compared VHA facilities with commercial managed care systems in 7 measures of diabetes treatment;[3]
- The Rand Corporation concluded its 'Comparison of Quality of Care for Patients in the Veterans Health Administration and Patients in a National Sample' by finding that the VHA outperforms all other sectors of American healthcare in 294 quality measures;[4]
- Medical Care in 2006 published a study comparing life expectancies of elderly patients in the VA to Medicare Advantage beneficiaries and concluded that Medicare Advantage mortality rates were 'significantly higher' than VHA;[5]
- The National Committee on Quality Assurance ranks health plans on performance measures such as high blood pressure management and adherence to protocols of evidence-based medicine. In the NCQA 2004 State of Health Quality report, the VHA outperformed all other medical systems including Johns Hopkins, the Mayo Clinic and Massachusetts General Hospital. 'In every single category, the veterans healthcare system outperformed the highest-rated non-VA hospitals' according to VHA researcher Phillip Longman.[6]

- According to 2005 VHA data, 69% of patients are seen by their physicians within 20 minutes of their scheduled appointment and 93% see specialists within 30 days of their desired appointment time[7]. As a result, for the past 6 years the VA has outranked private-sector hospitals on patient satisfaction in the annual consumer survey conducted by the National Quality Research Center at the University of Michigan.

Some Canadians see the VA as a model healthcare system. Canadians 'are struggling with the issue of 'sustainability.' The transformation of the Veterans Health Administration suggests that the key to sustainability is not levels of spending per se but public confidence that a system delivers value for money. The VHA regained confidence by defining its value (quality) and being accountable for delivering it.'[8]

Not only does the VHA offer better quality and customer satisfaction than commercial American healthcare, but it also costs less. From 1995—2004 the Medical Consumer Price index rose 39%; Medicare's cost per patient rose 40%; but the VHA's cost per patient rose only 0.8%. Between 1995—2003, the VA increased the number of patients treated on an annual basis by 75% (from 2.8 to 4.9 million) with only a 32% cumulative increase in its budget. And while increasing patient treatments, it reduced its hospital and long term care beds from 92,000 to 53,000 and increased its outpatient clinics from 200—850.[9]

Interestingly, some 60% of VHA recipients (1992 data) had no private or Medigap insurance, so used the VHA as their main or only health coverage. As many of these vets were low income, psychologically and economically disadvantaged people, this made the VHA a national safety net for veterans.[10]

In 2004, the average American consumed $6,280 of healthcare, but the VHA spent an average of only $5,562 per patient. Remember that veterans in the VHA system are, as a group 'far older, sicker, poorer and more prone to mental illness, homelessness and substance abuse than the population as a whole. Half of all VA enrollees are over age 65. More than a third smoke. One in 5 veterans has diabetes compared with 1 in 14 US residents in general. Name any chronic disease—Alzheimer's, cancer, congestive heart failure, sclerosis of the liver—and a much higher percentage of veterans have it than do Americans in general'[11] (Note that some savings result from closing obsolete VA facilities and many VA enrollees get some benefits elsewhere. But the trend is clear.)

Jonathan Perlin, acting undersecretary for health summarized the VA experience: 'If we've proved anything...in the last 10 years, it is that quality is less expensive.'[11]

The VHA is a huge organization, employing over 198,000 people, managing 154 hospitals and 875 clinics, and serving 5.4 million patients.[12] Interestingly, it also has a lifetime relationship with its patients so has incentives for investing in prevention and effective treatment, rather than simply billing for services rendered.

How does the VHA achieve these remarkable quality results with this frail population at lower costs than the private sector? First, the VHA has a clear definition of value: 'a balanced performance of five factors: cost, access, technical quality, patient functional ability and patient satisfaction' according to Ken Kizer, former VHA Undersecretary for Health.[13] Second, the VHA has two distinctive systemic features: its information technology system and its incentive structure.

VHA Information Technology: VistA

All VA facilities use a state of the art electronic medical records system, as opposed to BusinessWeek's estimate of only 20% of civilian hospitals. The VHA uses its own, internally designed VistA information system. VistA is a bundle of over 20,000 software programs written primarily in the 1970s and 80s by individual VA physicians and other VA professionals, generally in their spare time. The system was not designed by IT consultants working with VA administrators; it was engineered as a 'bottom-up' system.

VistA is also 'open source' software, which allows registered users to improve or adjust programs as needed. This program has 'dramatically reduced medical errors at the VA while also vastly improving diagnoses, quality of care, scientific understanding of the human body, and the development of medical protocols based on hard data about what drugs and procedures work best...the only function VistA can't do as well as its private sector counterparts, at least without adding some code, is tracking patient billing' according to Longman.[14]

Quick history of VistA. In the 1960s, the VA Office of Data Management and Telecommunications had a 17 step bureaucratic process that took about 3 years for approving new software. It was main-frame based. But the mini-computer revolution of the 1970s took power from huge mainframes and put it in lower, more operational levels of the bureaucracy.

Physicians and VA employees began writing their own mini-computer based programs to solve their operational problems because the VA bureaucracy was so ineffective. The VA's Computer Assisted System Staff somewhat covertly coordinated this mini-computer effort and persuaded users to share a common, user-friendly, open source language.

By 1981 this underground effort was sufficiently widespread that the VA's Chief Medical Director, Dr. Donald Custis, looked favorably on it, as did the Reagan administration. They supported VistA development over the previous mainframe operations.

VistA addressed issues that were not, then, typically facing commercial American health carriers or hospitals, but that would soon affect us all. The core problem: dealing with an elderly population presenting with numerous comorbidities and chronic conditions. VHA patients—far more than the general American public then—presented with diabetes, high blood pressure and cardiovascular disease (among others) that required constant monitoring and coordinated care from specialists, nurses, radiologists, lab workers, physical therapists and counselors.

(These chronic conditions became more prevalent in the general population a couple decades later, fuelled largely by the obesity epidemic and the medical successes of treating many episodic problems. See Chapter 4 on 'Ineffective Chronic Disease Care' for more on this.)

The frail VA population needed exceptionally good record keeping both to schedule medicines and tests and to monitor results. Since the VHA operated on a fixed budget with an increasing population, it also needed exceptionally good data on which treatments worked and which didn't.

The VA faced a second IT problem in the 1970s and 80s that the US commercial healthcare system has not yet solved. VA beneficiaries could move from city to city or state to state easily, but still needed access to their medical records. VistA needed to coordinate records among all VA facilities and offer patient data to all VA physicians.

Thus the VHA faced a unique set of problems. It had a long term / lifetime relationship with its beneficiaries, so could amortize an IT or chronic disease management program investment over time. 'From a very early data, both VA doctors and administrators were far more likely than their private-sector counterparts to see the value of investing in information technology that could improve the practice of medicine' suggests Longman.[15]

VistA keeps complete medical records of patients, including daily weight fluctuations, medications, daily blood pressure and other data. This is available to physicians—and increasingly patients—on laptops or PDAs. VistA allows viewers to graph data for easy viewing. This availability of complete, easily accessible patient data allows the VA to manage patients particularly well:

1. **Chronic disease management:** Oncologists, for example, can follow blood patient blood counts over time. Click a box and get a graph to see patient progress with a particular treatment. 'In the field of oncology,' according to Dr. Steven Krasnow of the Washington VA Medical Center, 'following blood counts of patients over time is very important. And the ability to essentially click one box and show a graph of the patient's individual blood count has been invaluable in maintaining patient safety and providing guidance to the clinician.'[16] (Neither Harvard affiliated teaching hospital that treated my wife in 2007 and 2008 had an IT system with this graphing ability.)

   The Baltimore VA reports a vast improvement in cancer screening rates. In 1990 rates of screening for breast and cervical cancer were 50 and 17%, respectively. By 2003 they were 88 and 87%. The computers drive this performance according to Dorothy Snow, acting chief of staff at the Baltimore VA hospital. [17]

2. **Prevent medical errors:** VistA eliminates handwritten physician scripts and the potential confusion between, for example, thioridazine and thiothixene. It also eliminates inappropriate Rx combinations as it keeps track of patient allergies and patient medications to eliminate contraindications.

   The VA also, interestingly, bar codes all medications and requires all patients to wear bar coded bracelets. The patient's code includes name, types of medication required, dosage, name of nurse authorized to administer the medications and medication timing. Before administering medication, the nurse scans the patient bracelet, his/her own bracelet and the medication bar code. This has virtually eliminated medication dispensing errors in the VA; but few commercial hospitals have such a structure. (The Harvard affiliated teaching hospitals my wife visited in 2007 and 8 did not have this system in place.) More on safety, below.

3. **Efficiency gains:** Easy access to all patient data on a physician's laptop eliminates the need to run around the hospital retrieving medical records—X-rays from radiology, lab results from the basement, etc. One neurologist practicing at both Georgetown University Hospital and the Washington VA Medical Center reports that he can see as many patients in a few hours at the VA as he can all day at Georgetown.[18]

4. **Patient and family access to records:** Patients can access their own records from their home computer, or grant permission for someone else to so access. This allows a child in, say, Massachusetts to help a geriatric VA parent in Florida to take the right medications. And it allows patients to refill their own prescriptions electronically and track their personal health information such as blood pressure and blood sugar levels.

5. **Scheduling:** VistA reminds patients to make appointments and to take their medications.

6. **Measurable results:** The VA estimates that VistA has saved 6000 lives since introduction by improving rates of pneumonia vaccination; the vaccination rate went from 29% in 1995 to 94% in 2005. The results: 4000 fewer hospitalizations and a $40 million annual savings.[19]

7. **Education and research gains:** VistA can review thousands of medical records quickly. This allows researchers to see treatment variations and results among diabetics, for example, by location, physician and treatment. This allows for treatment protocols based on hard data, rather than, as is often the case, on factors such as where a doctor when to medical school or on highly variable local traditions of care. [20] This also allows researchers to create the first national, risk-adjusted analysis of how patients fare after undergoing different types of surgery in different veterans

hospitals. And it shows which surgical teams, for example, have outstanding results and which need improvement.

8. **Management tool:** VistA allows managers to actually 'manage healthcare'. What percentage, for example, of VA patients by age (location?) get prostate screenings? How long do patients wait for an appointment? How often do medical errors occur and what are their patterns?

9. **Safety:** The VistA bar code system has virtually eliminated dispensing errors. The VA estimates that it prevented some 549,000 errors between 1994 and 2001. This includes a 75% decrease in errors involving the wrong medication; 62% decrease in errors involving wrong dosage; 93% reduction in the wrong patient receiving medication and 70% reduction in number of times a nurse simply forgot—or was too busy to—give patients their meds. The net result: while some 3— 8% of the nations prescriptions are filled incorrectly, the VA's prescription accuracy rate is greater than 99.997%.[21]

    'They've adopted a culture of patient safety and quality that is pervasive,' says Karen Davis, president of the Commonwealth Fund that studies healthcare issues.[22]

10. **Uniformity of care.** The VHA uses its extensive data base to determine appropriate care for each patient and monitors treatments by condition and location. Dorothy Snow, acting chief of staff at the VHA in Baltimore reviews weekly statistics on how her facility compares with on various measures. This helps maintain uniform practices and cost equalization throughout the VHA system.

    Compare that efficiency to Medicare. Patients in their last 6 months of life at New York's Mount Sinai Medical Center received an average 53.9 doctors visits, while similar patients at Duke University Medical Center received only 20.9. Yet all those extra doctors' visits at Mount Sinai add no gains to life expectancy—just higher medical bills.[23]

11. **Efficiency:** BusinessWeek estimates that 96% of VA prescriptions and medical orders are entered electronically,

compared to about 8% commercially. 'One out of five tests in a civilian hospital have to be repeated because the paper results are lost' according to Veterans Affairs Secretary R. James Nicholson. 'That's not happening in our hospitals.' Which may explain the high level of customer satisfaction.

Interestingly, acting undersecretary Perlin estimates that it costs the VA about $87 per patient per year to operate electronic health records, 'roughly the equivalent of not repeating one blood test.' [24]

With these excellent results from the VistA system, why don't commercial US hospitals—or Medicare—simply install it? There are several answers.

First, the economics of competitive commercial hospitals and insurance carriers dictate against paradigmatic IT investments. Such an investment has huge up-front costs that will negatively affect the hospital's cash flow or the carriers' premiums. Remember that perhaps 20% of a carrier's current subscribers will switch to a different carrier next year. Why should a carrier raise its premiums to invest in these people, only to make them healthier for their competitor when they switch next year—for lower premiums?

Hospitals also fear—economically—that providing more efficient and effective treatment will reduce their occupancy rates, thus additionally harming cash flow.

Second, the US lags other countries in applying information technology to healthcare nationally.[25] Germany, for example, began investing in a national IT healthcare information network in the 1990s and spent $1.88 billion or $21 per capita on this by 2005. By contrast, the US has spent $.43 per capita. Without the necessary massive national infrastructure, much of VistA's power is inapplicable.

Interestingly, many other countries have adopted VistA—including Finland, Germany, Nigeria, Mexico, India, Pakistan and Uganda.[26] There is even an Arabic language version up and running in Egypt.[27] Dr. Ian Reinecke of Australia's electronic medical records program—who has even recruited VA officials to work with him—says 'the US Veterans Health Administration is regarded as one of the best and most successful e-health systems in the world.'[28] But VHA officials reported in 2005 that they were unaware of any private healthcare system in the US using VistA—even though it's available for free on the internet. [29]

VA Incentive Structure

The VA's lifetime relationship with patients creates a different economic focus from the private sectors'. For the VA, investing in chronic disease control could mean huge future savings; for the private sector, investing in chronic disease control means huge short term costs.

Thus the VA has an incentive to invest in prevention and chronic disease management, whereas the private sector has incentives to bill fee-for-service excessively. We saw the problems this poses with Manhattan's Beth Israel Medical Center's diabetes program. The hospital lost money as the program succeeded and patients improved.

Kenneth Kizer, head of the VA under President Clinton, summarized this impact on pharmaceutical choice:

> If you know you're going to have your patients for five years, ten years, 15 years or life, there are good economic and health reasons why you would want to use these more expensive drugs. You have a population of patients who are at high risk for sclerotic heart disease, and you have them for life. You make different decisions about what's on your formulary than you might if you only had them for a year or two.[30]

The VA uses its VistA system to determine which drugs work best and then—unlike Medicare—negotiates with pharmaceutical companies. Interestingly, the VA does not rely on pharmaceutical-funded research that may reflect private company incentives, such as showing that 'new and more expensive' drugs are better than old. No other US hospital system has both this long term patient focus and objective medication results data.

One result: the consumer group Families USA estimates that VA patients pay, on average, 46% less that Medicare Part D enrollees for the same medications.[31]

***

The VA's VistA system and long term focus work to make this an outstanding healthcare system. Let's review our 6 American healthcare problems and see how the VHA stacks up.

1. **Uninsured.** The VA used to insure all veterans. It now only provides long term healthcare for those able to show 'combat related problems.' This is very unfortunate.

2. **The Medical Arms Race.** Here the centralized VA administration helps make rational technology purchases. The VA administration can use outcome data from VistA when evaluating technology options.

3. **Moral hazard.** The VA incentive structure plus outcome data has largely eliminated moral hazard as a concern.

4. **Chronic disease care and prevention.** The VA is outstanding at preventing and treating chronic conditions.

5. **Uneven treatment quality nationally.** Here VistA helps administrators compare results data to ensure that all veterans receive the same, evidence-based, high quality care.

6. **Quality and safety.** The VA beats all commercial healthcare systems in its quality and safety results.

Based on these outstanding results, should we expand the VA to handle all healthcare for all Americans? Probably not, for several reasons. **First,** the VA eligibility guidelines have been tightened since 1996. No longer do all veterans receive comprehensive medical services for life. Rather, new VA members only receive long-term medical services for 'combat related' problems. This eligibility tightening corresponded with Medicare's expansion into prescription drugs. There is an apparent political willingness to expand Medicare's inefficient programs, rather than the VA's efficient ones. Perhaps this is due to Medicare's allowance for Congressional meddling, or perhaps to other political pressures.

Second, veterans share special bonds together that non-veterans do not share. One reason the VHA works so well is its shared value relationship with its clients. 'For this reason, I've come to believe that it would not be a good idea to allow people who have no connection to the military to have access to VA hospitals' concludes Phillip Longman in his analysis of the VHA system.[32] Indeed, in 1992 when the then-VA secretary Edward Derwinski suggested allowing non-vets into 3 underused VHA hospitals, veterans groups forced his resignation.

Third, the VHA works well due to the combination of VistA and long term incentives. Altering the model to include a fee-for-service component, or including patients with 1 year insurance policies (not lifetime) would radically change this system.

Fourth, simply copying the VHA management structure and VistA onto the existing US commercial provider system runs into the same problems as copying Canadian medicare: lack of systemic evolution. As the VHA evolved, various provider groups 'bought in' to the operation and allowed the process to continue. Absent this buy in (and often even with it) the VHA faced resistance due to its bureaucratic structure. Even if we could figure out how to transition from our existing healthcare system to a national VHA-type—no small task!—we would still face the enormous bureaucratic acceptance problem. In short, transforming the $2 trillion US medical economy according to the VHA model—or any other blueprint—seems a managerial impossibility.

And that begs the question of whether Congress would agree to stop meddling!

Fifth, much of the current VHA success has come from brilliant management, particularly under Kenneth Kizer. In contrast to Medicare for example, the VHA is an integrated delivery system with salaried physicians and coordinated care. But 'we were an integrated delivery system before and no one said we had an advantage' then, claims undersecretary Perlin.[33]

It's unclear that Kizer's successors will be equally able. Dr. Dennis O'Leary, president of the Joint Commission on Accreditation of Healthcare Organizations warns that 'the most common reason hospitals go into the tank is a change in leadership.'[34] Since the VA is always affected by politics, this is an on-going concern he says.

And remember Robert Michel's Iron Law of Oligarchy that reform movements end when administrators and bureaucrats take over. We have not yet, in the US government, found a mechanism for ensuring continued creativity and reform, but we have plenty of examples of calcified administration that blocks creative and reforming programs.

Just look at the VHA's initial response to VistA. It's unclear that the VHA will continue to innovate and remain a healthcare leader in the future. It's unclear that the VHA will continue to innovate and remain a healthcare leader in the future. It may—but there is no structural reason to believe that it will.

CHAPTER 11:
Should We Turn to True Managed Care?

Managed Care delivers healthcare through competing large Integrated Delivery Systems, a.k.a. Prepaid Group Practices or Health Maintenance Organizations.

An alternative to single payer healthcare is managed care, sometimes known as managed competition or prepaid group practices. Under managed care, large multispecialty group practices provide a comprehensive set of healthcare services at a per capita price set in advance.[1] These large practices compete with each other to provide the best value to subscribers.[2] Members of one prepaid group practice could use all facilities of that practice, but none of a competitor. Each local hospital, for example, would join only one prepaid practice.

As envisioned by perhaps its foremost proponent Alain Enthoven, Professor Emeritus at Stanford Business School, managed care organizations are integrated entities that include both healthcare delivery systems (providers, labs, etc) and an insurance (financing) function. The critical components are:

1. Multispecialty group practices, comprised of primary care physicians, nurses, specialists, etc, who can serve the entire local community;
2. A voluntarily enrolled population that understands the advantages (price and hopefully quality) and disadvantages (reduced provider choice) of membership;
3. Comprehensive care;
4. Per capita prepayment;
5. Accountability by the organization; and
6. A close relationship between the financial and healthcare service delivery arms.[3]

The goal of managed competition, according to Enthoven is 'to divide providers in each community into competing economic units and to use market forces to motivate them to develop efficient delivery systems.' Only through competition can the health plans that do the best job of improving quality, cutting costs and satisfying patients be rewarded. Competition occurs at the level of integrated financing and delivery plans, not at the individual provider level.

This environment will force competing prepaid group practices to innovate and improve care quality while reducing costs. As such it is far superior to single payer healthcare which has no such competition forcing innovation and cost control. For managed care / managed competition to work, perfect premium price competition among plans must be preserved. Any interference with price competition—including government practices, taxes, union demands or other artificial market imperfections—will modify the competition and reduce its positive effects.

Prepaid group practices originally developed through competition with the traditional fee-for-service / indemnity coverage. To survive, the flagships of the HMO movement had to outperform traditional medical practices. These original groups included Group Health Association in DC (founded in 1935), Group Health Cooperative of Puget Sound (founded in 1945) and Kaiser Permanente (founded in the 1930s) the largest of all. Kaiser is generally regarded as the prime model of a successful prepaid group practice.

A LOOK AT KAISER PERMANENTE: Kaiser Permanente was formed in the 1930s when industrialist Henry Kaiser contracted with physician / entrepreneur Sidney Garfield to provide healthcare to Kaiser employees. Garfield owned a small chain of health clinics. For $.05 per employee per day he offered to cover industrial medical care (workers comp), and for an additional $.05, non-industrial healthcare (major medical) for all Kaiser employees.

As this business grew, Garfield contracted with the Permanente medical group. Kaiser became Permanente's exclusive client, and Permanente, Kaiser's exclusive provider. The organization became known as Kaiser-Permanente.

KP owned its own hospitals to eliminate the conflict between hospitals wanting higher occupancy and carriers wanting lower. Physicians were salaried employees. KP emphasized prevention, for they had incentives to keep people healthy and out of the hospital. As the company grew, it innovated to maintain quality while reducing costs:

1. Kaiser hospitals in the 1950s reported 25% shorter stays than the US hospital average;
2. Kaiser's ratio of outpatient visits to hospital admissions was 50% higher than the US average in 1969;
3. In the 1960s, Kaiser was among the first to offer home nursing services as a substitute to expensive lengthy hospitalizations;
4. Through the 1970s and 80s, Kaiser continued to emphasize outpatient care, becoming one of the first institutions to offer freestanding surgery and emergency care facilities.[4]

In 1971, Dr. Cecil Cutting, the executive director of the Kaiser Permanente Medical Group in northern California wrote that the 'direct relationship of prepayment to providers become an incentive for the physician to develop economies in spending the medical dollar while maintaining quality.'[5]

Kaiser Permanente developed a unique institutional culture, emphasizing prevention, waste reduction and a constant search for the least expensive / best treatment option.[6] Much of this came from Sidney Garfield. His waste control fanaticism became legendary: employees could only get a new pencil if they turned in a pencil stub of less than 3 inches. 'This period of stringent economy established a pattern of frugal allocation of resources that persisted even into more prosperous years' suggests Harvard's Regina Herzlinger.[7]

The Kaiser culture formed in opposition to—and under attacks from—organized medicine. Garfield established his medical operations in the Mojave Desert in the early 1930s. He battled Great Depression economics and organized medicine that viewed his physicians as an economic threat. (Independent medical practitioners worried that prepayment would motivate physicians to provide fewer services than needed, thus harming both the profession's reputation and pocketbook.)

Garfield hired only true believers in his model, people interested in making the plan work. He claimed that 'if you don't have the [people] who have it in their hearts to make it work and who believe in prepaid practice, it won't work.'[9] His physicians worked 6 days per week. They formed tight social groups. 'We picked people who liked each other—we felt like we were enjoying outselves.'[8] Garfield worked alongside staff physicians and continually sought their input and new ideas. His clinics were dynamic worksites.

This bonding experience led to KPs' unique corporate culture. Kaiser developed its own unusual organization structure that integrated physicians, hospitals and insurance with each other, plus prepayment. These were innovative ideas at the time. In business terms, KP successfully vertically integrated the provider and financial functions for the overall good of the organization—very difficult to do. (See discussion of vertical integration and transfer prices, below.)

NIXON'S HMO LAW OF 1973: Richard Nixon used Kaiser-Permanente as the basis of his HMO Law of 1973, as KP was the largest and most successful of the HMO models. Unfortunately, Nixon's legislation changed enough key elements so the final product varied significantly from its KP roots.

First, under Nixon's law, HMO meant simply 'prepayment'—not vertical integration. So healthcare delivery and healthcare finance were separate functions, handled by separate companies. The key integration feature that made Kaiser-Permanente so successful was lost in the legislation.

Second, Nixon's law called for a loose physician structure, in which practitioners could opt in or out of any HMO. Again, the opposite of KPs tight structure, in which physicians were fully integrated into both the hospital and financial system. The loose physician structure meant that providers had no particular loyalty to any specific HMO. Another key feature of KP was lost.

Third, Kaiser-Permanente used a capitated financial structure to motivate providers to control costs. Nixon's law allowed providers to bill insurance carriers on a fee-for-service basis. Absent capitation, much of the underlying financial advantage disappeared.

Fourth, Nixon only budgeted $325 million to assist new HMOs over 5 years. Senator Ted Kennedy and Nixon's own Secretary of Health, Education and Welfare, Elliot Richardson had requested $3.9 billion. The $325 million proved insufficient to achieve the goals.

What were the results of Nixon's legislation? 'The HMO Act of 1973 clearly inhibited HMO development' claims Jan Coombs in *The Rise and Fall of HMOs*.[10] Some 124 HMOs developed from 1970—1974, but only 40 developed from 1974—1978. Also, the enticement of public funding was insufficient to overcome the legislative and regulatory requirements, so many HMOs turned to Wall Street financing. In 1981, 88% of HMOs were nonprofit; by 1986 this had fallen to 41%.

Yet HMO subscriptions grew because HMO premiums were lower than the alternative, indemnity coverage. As a result:

By 1980, 9 million Americans enrolled in HMOs;
By 1990, 33 million enrolled;
By 2000, 60 million enrolled.

COST AND QUALITY CONTROLS 1970—2000 Nixon's managed care legislation was supposed to control healthcare costs and improve quality. Unfortunately, the legislation differed so significantly from Kaiser Permanente's model that carriers and various government agencies had to step in and devise new cost and quality control mechanisms, previously unseen at KP or other managed care organizations. Many of these controls became codified in our healthcare operations and still continue today; they institutionalized a non-KP type of 'managed care.'

According to Northwestern Professor David Dranove, these cost and quality control programs 'utterly failed on all accounts.'[11] Just as Michels had predicted, bureaucrats and administrators—not physicians and medical practitioners—took over and sabotaged the managed care reform movement. They turned it into something that Sidney Garfield would not have recognized.

Hospital Cost Control Programs

New York State had developed the first rate setting program in 1970. The New York legislature tried to cap Medicaid hospital payments and included private carriers in the program to avoid hospital cost shifting. This system was already in place when Nixon's HMO legislation passed. It continued since Nixon's plan allowed hospitals to bill carriers fee-for-service.

The New York State Prospective Rate Setting System established a flat fee per patient per day. The fee was set at the beginning of each year so hospitals could budget and plan, and was approximately equal to the average cost per patient per day the previous year with an inflation factor and regional cost variations applied.

Hospitals quickly learned how to game the system. Since they received the <u>same reimbursement</u> from Medicaid for all patients, they <u>earned more</u> by admitting the healthy and denying care to the sick. Not a good solution.

New Jersey sought to improve on New York's model and introduced it's own Prospective Payment System in the late 1970s—a few years after Nixon's HMO legislation. New Jersey modified New York's calculation of average cost/patient/day by introducing some 470 Diagnosis Related Groups (DRGs). This system, designed by Yale Medical School, divided patient costs into diagnostic groups. Cancer surgery now received a higher reimbursement than a simple overnight observation.

Under the New Jersey plan, hospitals would receive appropriate payment for medical treatment, but no more; patients would receive necessary care, but no more; and medical cost inflation would be controlled, at least in theory. Again this changed the KP model: there were no DRGs in Garfield's original system. Medicare took the New Jersey system national in the mid-1980s.

How did hospitals control their costs? Many shifted to more outpatient surgeries—not necessarily a bad thing. In 1984 some 28% of all community hospital surgeries were outpatient; by 1996 that percentage had increased to 59%, mirroring KPs experience.

Other hospitals simply managed their DRGs. Some hospitals hired DRG experts to help 'up-classify' patients to receive higher reimbursements. Others began 'dumping' expensive patients who exceeded their DRG reimbursements, by transferring them to other hospitals—presumably with less sophisticated admissions procedures. Some hospitals practiced 'skimming', by admitting only potentially profitable patients. While still others engaged in 'unbundling' services, or requiring patients to make more hospital visits at higher reimbursements, often with no additional health benefits.

Perhaps the biggest effect of DRG imposition was a change in hospital culture. Hospitals previously were generally non-profits, funded by charitable contributions and cost-plus reimbursement. They faced little financial risk. Perhaps they were more inclined to negotiate cooperative financial arrangements with carriers. As Dranove says

> Until the early 1980s, the managers of nonprofit health care organizations were under little financial pressure. Market conditions enabled even badly managed hospitals to survive. Private insurers either paid whatever price the hospital charged or paid the hospital for its costs plus a predetermined profit margin...(hospitals) that provided unprofitable services or cared for the uninsured covered the expenses by charging higher prices to everyone else.[12]

Physicians had traditionally run hospitals, leaving administrators to manage bookkeeping, purchasing and other defined line functions. These physicians could, perhaps, have worked in vertically integrated operations.

But DRGs changed this. By putting hospitals at financial risk, DRGs put hospitals and carriers on a competitive collision course. If the hospital managed its DRGs better than the carrier, then it received higher reimbursements—and earned more money—at the carrier's expense. Alternately, if the carrier outmanaged the hospital, it made money at the hospital's expense. No longer was collaboration even possible—competition ruled.

Hospitals addressed this competition by hiring MBAs and granting them true management responsibility. This opened a Pandora's box. Once hospitals began hiring sophisticated MBAs and giving them true responsibility, DRG management became a profession. MBAs learned how to manage hospitals...and then began buying them.

MBAs saw three particularly attractive reasons to own hospitals. First, hospitals had good long term cash flow provided by the government and private carriers. Second, implementing sound business practices could control hospital expenses—something previously insufficiently widespread in non-profit hospitals. And third, hospitals could design sophisticated accounting and billing systems to increase profits.

So attractive were these opportunities that investor-owned systems acquired over 100 hospitals by 1975; 273 hospitals by 1980 and nearly 500 hospitals (plus 200 more under management contract) by 1985.[13] Today investor-owned hospital networks dominate the landscape, and companies such as Partners Community Health Plan in Boston and the

Sutter system in California 'are unabashed about flaunting their power, publicly stating their intention to use their leverage when negotiating rates with managed care purchasers.'[14]

The DRG subtle accounting change altered the mindset of hospital administrators and investors and began our national shift to investor-owned and professionally managed hospitals. Hospitals felt they <u>had</u> to maintain control over their billing function. Though regulators won some DRG battles, within 25 years hospitals won the DRG war.

The loser: true managed care. Rather than developing a national system of integrated financing-treatment operations, we instead became an investor-owned, private hospital based healthcare system skilled at competing with financing organizations. The unintended consequence of Nixon's legislation became a stronger, more ingrained fee-for-service reimbursement system based on hospital-HMO competition. This was not at all what Sidney Garfield had originally developed.

Hospital Quality Control Programs

As Diagnosis Related Groups were aimed at controlling hospital costs, so various measures were introduced in the 1970s to control hospital quality. These aimed primarily at ensuring that patients received appropriate, high quality hospitalization and care.

They fared no better than DRGs and none supported close cooperation between carriers and hospitals.

The first Professional Standard Review Organizations (PSROs) began in 1972. These were established by the Social Security Amendments of 1972 to 'promote the effective, efficient, and economical delivery of health care services of proper quality for which payments may be made.'[15] PSROs were local physician organizations designed to monitor the necessity, appropriateness and quality of hospital care. PSROs established standards of care for a wide range of diseases, with a goal of treatment practice uniformity—rather like guilds.

These organizations were quite ineffective. Dranove suggests that local physicians were generally reluctant to punish their colleagues. PSROs created dilemmas for physicians who observed poor quality or excessive treatment in others. Should they report on physicians who unnecessarily bring patients into the hospital—but increase everyone's income? Should they be team players? Or should they fight other physicians and hospital administrators and create problems for themselves? Most physicians decided their interests—financial and professional—lay in getting along with their colleagues rather than reporting on them.

Regulators grasped this problem and modified the PSRO concept when creating the next quality control mechanism, the Professional Review Organization (PRO) in 1983. These were private companies, initially contracted by Medicaid. PROs were designed to assure the necessity and appropriateness of Medicaid services by reviewing hospital records for evidence of upcoding, dumping or unbundling of services. PROs established elaborate guidelines and enforcement protocols, again focusing on physicians and hospitals working in a particular locale.

Unfortunately, the process of developing guidelines introduced an even bigger problem—startling variations in medical practice across seemingly similar communities.[16] A famous early study 'Are Hospital Services Rationed in New Haven or Over-Utilized in Boston' reported that rates of certain procedures including coronary artery bypass graft surgery were much higher in New Haven than Boston, but rates of other procedures such as carotid endarterectomy were higher in Boston than New Haven.[17]

Studies such as this [18] suggested the PRO focus was too narrow and that the real hospital quality problem involved treatment variations. These put patients at risk, for some were under-treated while others were over-treated.

Such data spurred development of Treatment Guidelines, with a goal of standardizing medical treatments to control both quality and costs. Treatment guidelines typically provide the medical staff with detailed day-by-day instructions for testing, nursing, surgery, rehabilitation and discharge planning. Guidelines also provide a systemized method of ordering tests.

Unfortunately, contradictory treatment guidelines proliferated. By 1994 the AMA reported over 1600 sets of guidelines designed by (potentially) competing special interests. Hospital guidelines said 'treat' but carrier guidelines said 'don't treat'. Some guidelines were developed by pharmaceuticals and recommended drug therapy; others by surgical supply manufacturers and recommended surgery. Hospital bureaucracies and physicians resisted the imposition of guidelines, which ultimately became voluntary and only marginally effective.

Regulators next turned to Utilization Review to overcome the narrow focus of PROs and ambiguity of Treatment Guidelines.

Utilization Review is a screening procedure to determine (a) if the patient should be admitted, (b) surgical second opinions and (c) on-going review of high cost cases.

Independent 'objective' companies perform Utilization Review. These companies have developed best practice criteria. Procedurally, the hospital admissions nurse reports clinical data and a treatment plan to the UR nurse who may agree to hospitalization, recommend outpatient treatment or even refuse the treatment plan. Typically there is also an appeal procedure.

Supporters claim UR achieves two goals. First, UR companies keep their screens current with the medical literature, something no physician or hospital could possibly do with the hundreds of studies published annually. Second, they claim that UR reduces inpatient costs.[19]

Detractors see UR as an unwanted intrusion in the physician-patient relationship, with some physicians even lying to get around UR restrictions.[20] Other detractors claim the UR companies have a financial bias to show cost reductions in order to get their contracts renewed. Interestingly this is the opposite of hospitals' financial bias to perform treatments.

Some commentators have concluded that UR has failed to provide the desired level of cost and quality control. The Journal of the American Medical Association reported a 'Retrospective Drug Utilization Review' study in 2003 that concluded 'we were unable to identify an effect of retrospective drug utilization review on…clinical outcomes'[21]. The New England Journal of Medicine reported that a studied utilization review program 'reduced the number of diagnostic and surgical procedures performed that required second opinions…(but) otherwise the program had little effect'[22]. The Canadian Medical Association Journal published a research study 'How valid are utilization review tools in assessing appropriate use of acute care beds?' and found that some UR companies underestimate—while others overestimate—appropriate hospital admission stays.[23] The CMAJ article concluded that

> Although utilization review tools are widely accepted, these considerations…raise serious questions about the value of the tools… and whether they should be used at all.

Effects of Cost and Quality Control Programs on Managed Care Development

Some carriers like Utilization Review while others do not. But that misses our point. PROs, treatment guidelines and UR all fall outside the original Kaiser Permanente model and none induce a close, cooperative working relationship between carriers and hospitals. None, in other words, mitigate the conflict wrought by DRGs. But all became codified in US healthcare practices post-Nixon. All supported the deviation from true managed care. And all—especially when combined with DRGs—make a return to real 'managed care' a la Kaiser-Permanente increasingly difficult. The reason: to implement true managed care now, we must first undo all the post-1973 healthcare systemic and bureaucratic evolution based largely on conflict between hospitals and carriers. No small task.

Our 1973—2000 experience with managed care did, however, superficially appear somewhat successful. Healthcare spending in 2000 was $300 billion less than had been forecast by the Congressional Budget Office only 7 years earlier.[24] Unfortunately these savings were primarily the result of two features, neither of which appeared in the original managed care plan design:

1. Hospital overcapacity in the 1990s (resulting from overbuilding in the 1980s plus treatment constraints in the 1990s) allowed carriers to gain significant price concessions from providers;
2. Managed care insurance companies controlled costs by service denial: denial of provider payments, denial of specialist referrals, denial of hospital admissions. 'At the peak of managed care's sway, in 1999, far more physicians were financially rewarded for productivity [i.e. quantity of patient's seen] by insurers than for patient satisfaction' claims Harvard's Herzlinger. [25]

Providers hated managed care. Carriers squeezed hospital revenue. Physicians lost control of their incomes and professional independence—in both cases to administrators—largely because of DRGs and Utilization Review. Subscribers hated it for they felt at the mercy of a heartless insurance carrier that denied necessary services for the sake of profit. The popular 2002 film John Q played on these concerns—a father whose insurance company wouldn't pay for his son's medical treatments takes an Emergency Room hostage until doctors agree to operate. John Q could be any American according to the film's marketing; it grossed over $71 million in the first 2 months.

Meanwhile, the US Institute of Medicine in 2001, during the heyday of managed care, released its shattering study 'Crossing the Quality Chasm' claiming

> The US healthcare system does not provide consistent, high quality medical care to all people...between the healthcare that we now have and the healthcare that we could have lies not just a gap, but a chasm...

> The nation's healthcare delivery system has fallen far short in it's ability to translate knowledge into practice...

This and other observations led *The Economist* to claim that managed care just 'treated the symptoms'—like every other healthcare control strategy. 'What started as a revolution turn out to be mainly a mechanism for insurers to secure price discounts from physicians and hospitals.'[26]

THE MANAGED CARE PROPONENTS CALL FOUL: The US healthcare system that developed post 1973 was not the healthcare system envisioned or designed by true managed care proponents. It strayed from their original concept and KP's model, and thus failed to realize its true potential due to Nixon's political compromises and subsequent market evolution. The proponents called for a return to basics so managed care could finally replicate Kaiser Permanente's financial and quality results nationally; they did not want to be blamed for managed care's failure.

Thus Alain Enthoven wrote *The History and Principles of Managed Competition* and *Why Managed Care Has Failed to Contain Health Costs* both in 1993 [27] just as the Clinton administration began considering national healthcare reform...perhaps hoping that this time a President would bring his ideas to life. In these back-to-basics pieces Enthoven reminded readers that Nixon had perverted his ideal, creating 'a system dominated by the cost-increasing incentive of fee-for-service payment combined with the cost-unconscious demand of insured patients' whose insurance was paid by employers and subsidized by taxpayers.

US HMOs developed provider networks he claimed, simply by cobbling together independent physicians and paying them according to a fee schedule. This was not the Kaiser Permanente model!

Enthoven went on to decry fee-for-service for 11 reasons:

1. Fee-for-service creates an adversarial relationship between doctors and payers;
2. Fee-for-service has little accountability—poor data collection and provider motivations for economy;
3. Fee-for-service 'free choice of provider' leaves patients to make remarkably poorly informed choices;
4. Fee-for-service generates excess hospital capacity, high tech equipment and open-heart surgeries;
5. Fee-for-service generated an excess supply of specialists;
6. Fee-for-service misallocates resources, as no incentive to use the least costly settings for treatment;
7. Fee-for-service has no capacity to plan care processes from diagnosis to treatment to rehabilitation;
8. Fee-for-service has led to a dangerous proliferation of facilities for complex and costly procedures without the volumes necessary to maintain good outcomes;
9. Fee-for-service cannot practice total quality management due to lack of service integration;
10. Fee-for-service cannot organize the rational use of technology;
11. Organized systems, unlike fee-for-service, can emphasize prevention, early diagnosis and effective chronic disease management.

He further reiterated how to structure the market by a set of rules 'laid down once and for all.' These include appropriate types of plan sponsors, rules to ensure equity, rules to manage the enrollment process, rules for managing risk selection, rules for monitoring specialty care and quality, and lots more rules to make the system work. His goal: define a system involving

> Intelligent, active collective purchasing agents contracting with healthcare plans on behalf of a large group of subscribers and continuously structuring and adjusting the market to overcome attempts to avoid price competition.

Any deviation from this ideal system reduces its effectiveness. Groups that devised ways to get around the rules for their own advantage upset Enthoven. He lamented the self centered interests of many involved in healthcare: 'Whatever set of rules one proposes, critics could and did dream up ways for health plans to get around them to their advantage.' Welcome to capitalism, Professor Enthoven.

Nixon's HMO Law of 1973 and subsequent healthcare evolution so perverted his managed care ideal that he wrote in *Why Managed Care Has Failed to Contain Health Costs* 'Some say that competition has failed. I say that competition has not yet been tried.'

He described Health Insurance Purchasing Cooperatives as the mechanism of implementing true managed care, just as Hilary Clinton was developing her healthcare plan. Enthoven's *History and Principles* seemed to serve as the intellectual basis to promote true managed care for all.

The Clinton Administration did not pass its huge healthcare reform efforts. American culture and politics intervened, and for the second time in 20 years an attempt to take Kaiser Permanente national failed. Among the key reasons: 65% of respondents said 'being able to choose the medical services you want' was more important than 'controlling your costs for healthcare.'[28] The ensuing political debacle led to another 15+ years of fee-for-service healthcare that deviated from the 'true' managed care model, with economic and quality results that harmed Americans.

MANAGED CARE PROPONENTS CONTINUE TO BELIEVE: The true believers, though, weren't finished yet. In 2002, Enthoven and Laura Tollen edited 'Toward a 21st Century Health System' which again extolled the virtues of Kaiser Permanente. In the Foreword, William Roper, Dean of the University of North Carolina School of Public Health, claimed

> Prepaid group practices have remained the health reform prescription
> of choice of many in the health policy community...and I proudly
> put myself among them.

The problem with managed care in the 1980s-1990s, says Roper, was that it was forced on people, which planted the seeds of consumer backlash. Enthoven echoes this in his Preface by stating that 'Patient satisfaction depends a great deal on whether or not the patient became an HMO member voluntarily or involuntarily.' If only people would want to join prepaid group practices like Kaiser Permanente, then our healthcare system would improve. If only we could diffuse the model, then people would see its successes and want to join.

Chapter 1 of 'Toward a 21st Century...' discusses the two key barriers to diffusion of this model: lack of a group / corporate culture and lack of financial incentives.[29] Are these surmountable problems? Can the Kaiser Permanente model be successfully replicated? In other words, *can managed care ever work?*

The Corporate Culture Problem: By the late 1990s, Kaiser Permanente began losing money—some $270 million in 1997 alone. This was due to its rapid growth; some 50% of top managers were new to their positions by the late 1990s, and 20% of them were new to the organization. 'The culture-imbued physicians, the hospitals managed directly by Kaiser, the seasoned insurance officials who worked with the providers to balance healthcare quality and cost, the tense interplay among the three elements of the system—all were diminished' in this process, suggests Herzlinger. Kaiser's membership soared, but it nearly lost its soul in the process.[30]

Remember Sidney Garfield who claimed you need true believers to make prepaid group practices work. He went on to state that 'they aren't going to work unless they get men [and women] who really believe in giving service to the people.'[31] In a market based economy, it's very difficult to hire seasoned, experienced managers, skilled in competition but with the right care-giving, philosophical orientation.

Absent culture, HMOs manage costs by denying claims—not nearly the same as managing health. Even Enthoven agrees that developing a corporate culture takes time, energy and effort—they are 'difficult to develop and slow to grow'[32]—and then still may not succeed. Corporate culture grows from shared experiences and difficulties. You can't recreate Kaiser's culture without its evolutionary past. Absent soul and shared evolution, you're doomed to fail.

The Financial Incentive Problem, or Why Vertical Integration Fails: In Kaiser's model the providers and financiers work together for the overall good of patients and the organization. This is called vertical integration: the financial and provider functions belong to the same corporation.

Merging these functions together is extraordinarily difficult, especially absent the shared values of a meaningful corporate culture. Hospitals, physicians and financiers have fundamental conflicts:

- Hospitals want high bed occupancy to generate income; carriers want low occupancy to reduce expenses;
- Hospitals want high reimbursements per patient; carriers want low;
- Physicians want high compensation / rewards from hospitals for referrals; hospitals want to pay less
- Hospitals want to make money; carriers want to control premium rates

The financial mechanism that links the insurance function to the provider function is called a transfer price. If the transfer price is too high, then the insurance carrier loses money—a big problem if the insurance managers are compensated based on profits or if the insurance carrier is publicly traded.

If the transfer price is too low, then the hospital loses money—and hospital managers face the same problems.

If the transfer price is set at market, then why integrate? Remember Enthoven's 11 problems with fee-for-service pricing. At market transfer pricing, there seems little advantage to owning both the financial and delivery systems as you just recreate the problems that you integrated to solve.

Vertical integration, according to McKinsey 'is notoriously difficult to set, easy to get wrong and—when a company does get it wrong—very costly to fix.'[33] Enthoven apparently agrees, claiming the managing true prepaid group practices requires 'wise, if not visionary, leadership, which has been relatively rare in American healthcare in recent years.'[34]

The examples of good vertical integration in Prepaid Group Practices—Kaiser Permanente until the 1990s, Group Health Cooperative in Seattle, HealthPartners in Minneapolis, the Mayo Clinic in Minnesota and others—were formed in a different era. That was before hospitals consolidated, before universities trained students in healthcare administration, before American consumers became accustomed to wide provider choice and before the myriad of state and federal healthcare regulations. Senior officials at existing Prepaid Group Practices think that 'without substantial changes to the US financial and regulatory systems, it would be difficult for new PGPs to develop and for many of the current ones to expand' due largely to the difficulty of exporting the entrenched group culture.[35] In this, they are probably correct.

CAN MANAGED CARE WORK IN THE US TODAY? No, managed care cannot work in the US today; its time has passed. Even supporters see this, as Northwestern's Professor David Dranove wrote in 2002: 'my optimistic view of managed care's potential has wavered. I accept the possibility that managed care will never fulfill its promise.'[36] We had two major attempts to develop the Kaiser Permanente model as our national healthcare, and both Nixon and Clinton failed. It's time to move on.

I do not see the utility of comparing managed care / prepaid group practices to our 6 indicators of a good healthcare system. The simple reason: operationalizing managed care always changes the system so much as to make it virtually unrecognizable. We—real people in a real society—cannot implement the managed care ideal.

This is as Karl Popper suggested in Chapter 1. To implement Enthoven's idea successfully we must transform the nature of Americans to fit the model. With that as a precondition, managed care must fail.

But I see a curious trend in the literature. Even though managed care, as modeled by Kaiser Permanente, has failed to grow nationally, and even though our society has evolved, true believers still believe. Apparently no set of facts or circumstances can affect the faith that true believers have in that ideal.

Thus a PGP insurance executive describes the future of Organized Delivery Systems—another name for managed care: 'Organized healthcare in this country is going to increase. I think it is going to increase because we are heading toward the edge of a cliff...I think the only way we will be able to [deal with future healthcare issues] effectively is through organized delivery systems.'[37] Even though we can't figure out how to replicate Kaiser Permanente's model, despite 40 years of trying.

Or Berkeley's Professor Stephen Shortell quotes an old Scottish proverb: ' "There is no such thing as bad weather, only inappropriate clothing." Perhaps, some day, PGPs will be the appropriate "clothing" for dealing with the maelstroms of healthcare in America.'[38] Hardly a basis for good public policy. I wonder what set of facts might dissuade him of this belief?

This is eerily reminiscent of Arnold Relman from Chapter 5 who reviewed the evolution of healthcare in America, admits little chance that

America will embrace single payer healthcare in the foreseeable future, but remains 'convinced that a complete overhaul [toward a single payer system] is inevitable...'[39]

Single payer inevitability. Prepaid group practice as the prescription of choice. In spite of compelling arguments to the contrary, proponents hold their visions with almost religious fervor, seemingly ignoring contradictory evidence or opposing evolutionary trends in our healthcare system.

There is an interesting academic situation here. Virtually all single payer theorists use Canada or Medicare as their ideal model; they don't discuss either Kaiser Permanente or the RAND National Health Experiment research. By contrast, virtually all managed care theorists quote the RAND study extensively and use Kaiser as the idealized model, but rarely (never?) discuss Canada, Britain or Medicare. Surely each offers some useful lessons.

But 'true believer' theorists ignore evidence, evolution and experience, and write the same arguments over and over in a seemingly Sisyphisian effort to influence the direction of US healthcare.

Meanwhile the actual direction of our healthcare systemic evolves, ignoring these discussions. In the next chapter, we'll discuss the current evolutionary movement from botched managed care toward a more consumer oriented system. And we'll see if that may hold promise for long term healthcare improvement.

CHAPTER 12
The Consumerism Trend

This chapter describes four post-2000 trends toward increased consumerism in US healthcare.

Inflation returned post-2000 as the American healthcare marketplace evolved.

Many factors contributed, including consumer rebellion against HMO restrictions of the 1980s and 1990s—consumers demanded wider provider choice with fewer restrictions. Carriers responded by introducing new products offering wide choice of provider, higher deductibles and more copayments. Americans generally accepted this as private health insurance enrollments fell by only about 1.5%—from 201 million to 198 million -between 2000 and 2004.[1]

One effect of cost shifting: instill in consumer's minds that they pay for healthcare at the point of service. This further differentiated the American healthcare purchasing experience from Enthoven's paradigm of managed care.

The trend toward cost-shifting / consumer driven policies increasingly available after 2000 rests on 4 evolutionary legs: (1) commercial carrier plan designs, (2) President Bush's Health Savings Account legislation, (3) Massachusetts healthcare reform of 2006 and (4) the transparency movement.

<u>Commercial plan designs.</u> Post about 2000, commercial carriers increasingly shifted costs to consumers. Harvard Pilgrim Healthcare in Massachusetts, for example, introduced its Best Buy series of annual deductible plans post-2000, with deductibles ranging from $500—$2000. Customers apparently accepted these; by 2005 almost 20% of the Harvard Pilgrim policies we sold contained annual deductibles, compared to none prior to 2000.[2]

Also, in 2000 some 43% of our Harvard Pilgrim customers purchased the 'Premier' policy, which had no inpatient hospital copayment. By 2005 this percentage had decreased to 21%, indicating that the vast majority of our customers understood that patients pay at least something out-of-pocket for <u>hospitalizations</u>.

Final comparison: in 2000 only 14% of our Harvard Pilgrim sales were the 'Affordable' policies that had a $20 office visit copayment. By 2005, these policies represented 34% of our Harvard Pilgrim sales, indicating that consumers increasingly accepted out-of-pocket payments at <u>doctor's offices</u>.

Other carriers engaged in similar cost-shifting to consumers. By 2005 the vast majority of our customers accepted some element of cost-shifting as the quid-pro-quo of wider provider choice and fewer policy restrictions. Our experience mirrors the national trend.

The Feds Enhance This Process. President George W. Bush supported and enhanced this cost-shifting process by introducing Health Savings Accounts as part of the Medicare Modernization legislation of 2003. HSAs are specifically designed to make healthcare more like other economic goods and to inject more consumerism into healthcare purchases. HSA policyholders spend their own money (initially) on healthcare. According to the theory, this will induce them to shop more wisely, consider various treatment costs, avoid unnecessary procedures and lower our national healthcare inflation rate.

HSAs are comprised of two separate but linked components—a high deductible health insurance plan with an optional tax-advantaged savings account. The IRS defines 'high deductible health insurance plans' as having a maximum individual annual deductible of $2850 and family deductible of $5650 in 2007. The insured pays the entire deductible before the carrier pays anything. Once the insured reaches the annual deductible most or all medical services are fully covered by the carrier.[3]

The Health Savings Account legislation also allows policy subscribers to establish an optional, tax-advantaged 'health savings account'. HSAs look and act much like Individual Retirement Accounts. HSA investments can be pre-taxed (not included in the subscribers' adjusted gross income for tax purposes), accrue interest tax-free and be withdrawn tax-free, provided the funds are spent for IRS approved medical purposes.

Thus under HSA legislation, the healthcare premium deductibles now also become income tax-deductible, effectively saving the consumer about 1/3 in taxes.

To enhance consumer power, HSAs typically rest on a PPO, not HMO chassis. PPOs (Preferred Provider Networks) typically do not require referrals for in-network specialists. Instead of using referrals to control costs, HSAs use high deductibles.

Thus we see the beginning of a trend: healthcare inflation returned post-2000 largely due to consumer rebellion against HMO restrictions of the 1980s and 1990s. Carriers responded by cost-shifting to consumers. The Feds provided tax incentives to support this effort. By 2005 or so, most healthcare consumers (at least as evidenced by our agency) understood that significant copayments and deductibles had become a routine part of medical care—and that these will likely grow in the future. Indeed, the current state of 'health insurance budgeting and planning' for many small employers is to shift slightly more costs to employees each year.

Massachusetts Healthcare Reform Furthers This Process: In 2006, Massachusetts enacted healthcare reform designed to extend coverage to all state residents. Commentators called this 'truly significant and transformative' (Heritage Foundation) [4], 'far reaching' (New England Journal of Medicine) [5] and 'landmark' (Washington Post).[6] BusinessWeek wrote that 'Massachusetts may have broken the gridlock with an innovative bipartisan plan'[7] and the New England Journal of Medicine published a complementary article 'Can Massachusetts Lead the Way in Health Care Reform?'[8] claiming that 'many states are already taking a serious look at it's new plan' with an eye to copying it.

Massachusetts had about 6% uninsured prior to this reform. The legislation established two mandates: the 'individual mandate' requiring everyone in Massachusetts to have health coverage or face fines; and the 'employer mandate' requiring all businesses of a certain size to offer employer-sponsored health coverage or face other fines.

Massachusetts also established subsidy programs to reduce the financial burden of premiums on low and middle-income residents. Those earning less than 300% of the Federal Poverty Level (about $30,000 for an individual in 2007) would get state subsidies on a sliding income scale. They could use these subsidies to purchase a wide variety of commercial health insurance policies.[9]

Massachusetts induced health insurance carriers to design new 'Commonwealth Choice' products with the goal of making health insurance more affordable. Commonwealth Choice products comply with the same extensive state mandates as traditional commercial plans.

Carriers kept Commonwealth Choice plans 'affordable' by cost shifting to enrollees via high deductibles. Thus, for example, Harvard Pilgrim's Bronze Core Coverage has a $1500 deductible, Tufts Health Plan's Advantage HMO Select 2000 has a $2000 annual individual deductible, and Neighborhood Health Plan's Care Three Select charges 20% coinsurance after the $2000 individual annual deductible, up to $5000 per individual.

The Massachusetts carriers and state government decided to promote wide provider choice, relatively few provider restrictions, rich benefits and high deductibles. They could have designed plans differently with limited medical benefits or limited financial coverage. They also could have designed plans with small provider networks, high provider choice restrictions and low (no?) deductibles—much like Enthoven's idealized Integrated Delivery Systems. They could have designed multi-year plans. And they could have allowed consumers to choose among a range of different plan designs. But both the government and private carriers decided

1.   that limited network options were unattractive to consumers post 2006,
2.   that all plans must contain all state mandated benefits so consumers had virtually no discretion in benefit selection,
3.   that all plans would include 12 month only rate lock guarantees and
4.   that high deductibles were the best cost control option.

The underlying value here? That the government knows what's best for consumers. Massachusetts' health plans offer few real options as all plans include almost identical benefits and (with very few exceptions) use the same providers. The consumer's only choice: premium price, based largely on the amount of cost-sharing between the carrier and the consumer.

Thus, three evolutionary trends merge. **First**, in the face of consumer backlash about HMOs, commercial carriers cost shifted to subscribers while reducing plan restrictions. **Second**, President Bush provided tax benefits for purchase of high deductible plans. **Third**, Massachusetts' healthcare reform—perhaps a US model for insuring the uninsured—adopted high deductibles as its cost control mechanism of choice. These three trends led to a demand for <u>transparency</u>.

The Transparency Movement Transparency means making cost and outcome data available to consumers, thus making healthcare just like other consumer goods.

Transparency exists, for example, in the breakfast cereal market. We know what Corn Flakes cost—compared to Raisin Bran or Cheerios. We know what Post Corn Flakes cost compared to Kellogg or the store brand. We also know nutritional levels. Consumers can shop wisely for <u>value</u> based on costs and quality.

We do not, however, currently know what back surgery costs compared to other types of back treatment. (See Chapter 4 on back surgery rates in Fort Myers Florida compared to Dartmouth-Hitchcock Medical Center). Nor do we know what back surgery costs at one hospital compared to another. Nor do we have very good outcome data by treatment type or by provider.

Consumer-driven healthcare advocates see transparency as a necessary condition for value-based competition among healthcare providers—i.e. competition for the consumer's deductible dollars. A transparent system will allow consumers to chose the best <u>value</u> by comparing costs and outcomes for disease treatments among providers. Some consumers may opt for (more expensive) surgery—others for (less expensive) therapy. Some may chose (more expensive, perhaps state-of-the-art) surgery at a famous national hospital—others (less expensive, perhaps more routine) surgery at a local clinic.

Consumers, according to this theory, can make wise purchasing decisions by comparing costs and outcomes by procedure and by provider. This is a direct attack on moral hazard, the third healthcare problem discussed in Chapter 4.

Transparency became an increasingly discussed healthcare topic post-2000, stimulated in part by publication of several thoughtful business management books on healthcare. Among those:

- *Redefining Healthcare*, by Michael Porter (Harvard Business School) and Elizabeth Olmsted Teisberg (University of Virginia's Darden Graduate School of Business)[10];

- *Who Killed Healthcare*, by Regina Herzlinger (Harvard Business School).[11]

Massachusetts' government officials publicly began to discuss the need for transparency in 2007. Senate President Therese Murray, for example, in her October 24, 2007 speech to the Greater Boston Chamber of Commerce asks 'how do we make healthcare sustainable and affordable for the next 20 years?'[12] Part of her answer: 'require more public information and transparency...collect cost data and make it public.' Murray, a politician primarily concerned about the high cost of healthcare, discussed only the cost side—not the outcome side—in her speech. But even this kind of government support moves the transparency process forward.

Some Massachusetts carriers also seem to accept this. James Roosevelt Jr., President of Tufts Health Plan and Charles Baker, President of Harvard Pilgrim Health Plan echo Murray's call for transparency in their December 1, 2007 Boston Globe op-ed piece 'How to control healthcare costs'. They recommend public hearings on cost drivers and public reporting of healthcare revenues and expenses. Again they only discuss cost, not outcome reporting. This may be a first evolutionary step. After costs become publicly available, perhaps outcomes will follow.

Transparency becomes a fourth leg of healthcare evolution post-2000. **First** the carriers introduced deductible plans, **then** the Bush administration offered tax benefits for these plans, **then** the Massachusetts healthcare reform movement chose deductibles as it's cost control mechanism of choice. **Now** transparency comes along to help consumers decide how to spend their deductible dollars.

CHAPTER 13
CDHP—Consumer Driven Health Plans

Consumer driven health plans treat healthcare like other consumer goods and services.

What does an increasingly transparent, consumer oriented healthcare system resemble? According to Harvard's Regina Herzlinger, this looks like the retirement fund industry about 20 years ago, just as employees began to manage their own retirement savings. 'The current health insurance model resembles the way companies used to manage their employee's retirement savings. In traditional defined benefit plans, pension investments and returns were determined by employers; workers were given no choice, no control, and very little information.'[1]

Herzlinger has been described as the godmother of consumer driven healthcare by The American Spectator. She's America's leading advocate of market-driven, consumer-oriented health reform, according to the Economist. [2] Republican Congressman Paul Ryan claims that 'of all the thinkers on this topic, Regi has the most influence in Washington.'[3] Ron Williams, the Chairman of Aetna says that consumer driven healthcare is 'the most important trend to hit healthcare—and Regi is a beacon for us practitioners.'[4] Her books have been praised by Daniel Johnson (former President of the American Medical Association), Joseph Kennedy (President of Citizen's Energy), Paul Levy (CEO of Beth Israel Hospital, Boston), Peter Slavin (President of Massachusetts General Hospital) and US Senators Joseph Biden, William Frist, and Tom Coburn.

Herzlinger claims that once employees began to manage their own retirement savings, the market effects were 'dramatic and far-reaching.' **First,** the number and variety of investment options skyrocketed, so people could chose the retirement package that best fit their personality and needs. **Second,** sources of advice about retirement planning proliferated, including investment advisors and investment newsletters. **Third,** investors flocked to defined contribution plans compared to defined benefit plans; consumers exercised their muscle. And **fourth**, consumer pressure intensified competition and forced the entire US securities industry to become more customer oriented and efficient; financial transaction prices fell during the 1990s.

She believes that evolving healthcare consumerism will have the same impact on healthcare. This summary of consumer-driven healthcare is from a Harvard Business School 'Working Knowledge' interview:

> It is basically about giving us back the money we now hand over to our employers for health insurance, so we can buy our own. And if we're poor, the government will transfer money to us so that we can go and buy it for ourselves...

> The analogy is in the mutual fund market. Vanguard came along with the 401(k) and John Bogle, the amazing man who created Vanguard, knew that consumers were going to have to shop for retirement income choice, and what the hell would they buy? There were a lot of stinky products around. He created Vanguard and he created terrific products, these indexed mutual funds. Lots of employers picked up Vanguard, or Fidelity or T. Rowe Price, and they said 'We're not doing the investing for you anymore. We're giving you the money, and we're giving it to you in tax-sheltered ways so you can use your own money, and we're also giving you a great supermarket that has very good products in it.'

> The other part that the government must do is to require transparency, to require the quality metrics that we need in order to be good shoppers...

> I honestly believe that we will have it by the end of the term of the next President...we can transform ourselves with astonishing rapidity if we permit the transformative forces to work if we unleash consumers, unleash entrepreneurs, don't keep binding them up....

> The critical lever is getting the money to the consumers. [5]

In short, the consumer driven movement sees healthcare as a normal business service in our capitalist economy. Consumer driven theorists believe that the standard laws of business and economics apply to healthcare and the best type of healthcare system is one based on competition among providers. Market mechanisms, rather than government regulation, are the best way to improve our healthcare delivery system.

In the ideal consumer driven healthcare system:

Employees or individuals (acting either through their employer or directly to the carrier) will purchase health insurance and act to protect their own health status;

Entrepreneurial firms will supply the innovative insurance and information products that consumer driven healthcare programs require and will force status quo medical providers to innovate. Competition among them will continually improve products and reduce costs;

Government will subsidize the poor and oversee insurers and providers. It must not micromanage them and allow government bureaucrats to stifle innovation and prevent the creation of new consumer driven organizations and health insurance plans. [6]

Some Potential Effects of Healthcare Consumerism on Providers As consumers take on more and more healthcare decisions—in other words, as the four post-2000 trends develop—consumer advocates expect medical treatment prices to drop due to competition among providers. This echoes Hayek's suggestion that competition is a discovery procedure. Providers will try to treat patients better and less expensively—just as suppliers do in other industries—but differently from the traditional American 'medical guild' mindset.

Herzlinger believes that price competition will spur development of 'focused factories' to treat the most common medical problems, representing the bulk of our healthcare costs. Focused factories specialize in high volume procedures—for example, births, cataract surgeries or heart bypass operations—or specific medical conditions such as asthma, diabetes or cancer. The theory: [7]

1. A factory that focuses on a narrow product mix for a particular market niche will outperform the conventional plan which attempts a broader mission, thus generating better results;

2. The focused factory's equipment, supporting systems and procedures can concentrate on a limited task for one set of customers, so its costs are likely to be lower than a conventional plant;

3. Focused factories are surprisingly rare. Their antithesis, conventional factories—in our case, General Hospitals—produce many products for diverse customers, citing 'economies of scale' as justification;

4. The result, more often than not, is a hodge-podge of compromises with high overhead; an organization that is constantly in hot water with customers and inefficiently producing inferior products at higher prices.

Efficient healthcare providers should

1. Learn to focus on a limited, concise, manageable set of medical conditions, technologies, volumes and markets (patients);

2. Learn to structure their operations to focus on one explicit objective rather than many inconsistent, conflicting, implicit goals;

3. Define problems as encompassing the entire disease cycle from diagnosis to medical intervention to rehabilitation to follow-up, rather than on isolated treatment parts.

Medical focused factories are organized around patients' requirements, not provider convenience or academic medical department. 'They always contain all the resources needed…They provide expert specialists care for the other problems…It's comprehensive menu…[includes]…diagnosis, treatment, psychotherapy and financial counseling.' [8]

Herzlinger cites McDonald's as a focused factory example, claiming that McDonald's success rests on several bases:

1. **Outsourcing.** McDonald's provides clear specifications to suppliers, and then allows them to generate profits by working hard to meet McDonald's expectations. This is very different from Enthoven's vertically integrated model where everything

is done in-house—or today's horizontally integrated general hospitals—both with huge overheads. When outsourcing, McDonald's only pays overhead on the amount used: our general hospitals, by 'in-sourcing' pay 100% of the overhead, thus creating pressure for additional horizontal expansion;

2. **Investments in appropriate technology.** McDonald's designs technology specifically for it's very focused needs, thus producing better products at lower costs. McDonald's discovered, for example, that it's French Fries are perfectly produced when the oil temperature rises 3 degrees after the raw potatoes enter the hot oil. So it designed a cooking machine to achieve that result automatically;

3. **Investment in human resources.** By 1991 the McDonald's operations manual was 750 pages long, clearly defining every aspect of McDonald's operation. Remember that McDonald's just sells a limited menu of sandwiches, sides and drinks— much less complex than a hospital's medical treatments.

Compare McDonald's to this operating room description by Dr. Gerald Healy, President of the American College of Surgeons:

> The anesthesiologist, inexperienced in the procedure, was helpless… The regular nurses were unavailable, and their hastily selected replacements had never worked together…I found myself marooned, shouting a flurry of commands at a team too paralyzed to act.[9]

Or compare focused factories to today's healthcare, where a patient's care is provided in multiple sites—the PCP's office, various specialist's offices, the hospital ER, an outpatient site, an inpatient site, etc. No one provider is responsible for coordination, making the patient and/or family responsible for integrating all the appropriate information and care. Information may be lost and patient care may suffer. This system is extremely stressful on the patient and family—not nearly as convenient as it could be.

Focused medical factories would aim at specific medical problems, segment the market, bring down treatment costs, improve outcomes and offer the convenience currently lacking in US healthcare. Medical factories could focus on the handful of diseases and conditions that generate the bulk of US medical costs and thus have a significant impact on total US healthcare spending.

The $130+ billion direct costs of diabetes treatment, for example, could fund, on average in each state, one 500-bed hospital, five 200—299 bed hospitals, and 30 community facilities costing $10 million each—just for diabetes.[10] This could both improve treatment outcomes and reduce costs with the single disease focus and concomitant economies.

What would a diabetes focused factory look like? Manhattan's Beth Israel Medical Center's diabetes program—described in Chapter 4. Its program would include medical care, patient education, disease prevention and disease management—all run by a multi-disciplinary staff of nurses, dietitians, exercise physiologists, mental health professionals and various medical specialists (endocrinologists, nephrologists, podiatrists, cardiologists, etc). Patients would participate in

- Regular blood sugar monitoring
- Nutritional counseling
- Disease management sessions with teams of specialists
- Exercise programs and monitoring

These programs offer potentially enormous economic savings. Researchers estimate that more than 80% of women's coronary events could be prevented through exercising moderately, not smoking, maintaining a healthy weight and eating foods high in fiber and low in saturated or tans fats [11]—in other words, by following a Beth Israel type program. Joslin Diabetes Center reports that obese adults who lost 7% of their weight (about 16 pounds for a 220 pound person) and exercised moderately for six months improved their major blood vessel function as much as 80%—reducing need for future expensive acute medical interventions. Focused factories could produce the effective chronic disease care that our current system now lacks.

Similar situations exist around the other disease drivers of healthcare costs, including coronary procedures, back treatments, births and asthma. Six types of medical conditions accounted for 80% of all medical procedures performed at free-standing ambulatory surgical centers in 1991.[12] Performing these in a cost effective, safe and efficient focused factory that included prevention, treatment, rehabilitation and patient follow-up could have a major impact on US healthcare costs.

The Insurance Carrier's Role. Advocates of consumer-driven healthcare argue that increased consumer sovereignty will lead to major supply innovations. While we cannot exactly specify future consumer-driven insurance policies (because they will evolve as the market evolves), here are some potential scenarios: [13]

1. **Health insurance policies will offer integrated medical care.** Focused factory provider teams will quote prices for bundles of services. Consumer-driven policies will discard current DRG-based fragmented care and allow providers to take a more comprehensive approach to treatment, focused on outcomes, not processes.

2. **Insurance policies will address chronic diseases through multi-year policies** that will allow providers to emulate the Veterans Health Administration incentive structure. These will induce providers to take a long term view of patients and provide the best long term care, rather than (as today) the cheapest short term. This will include quality chronic care programs such as Manhattan's Beth Israel Hospital diabetes program described in Chapter 4.

3. **Insurance policies will offer different benefits over different time periods.** Carriers can offer different bundles of services and consumers can chose which to purchase. A 60 year old, for example, may want policies that include long term care benefits but not maternity; a 20 year old may want the opposite. A 30 year old may want a relatively short term policy to keep prices low while saving for a house downpayment. But a 50 year old may want to lock in rates for 10 years.

4. **Providers** will offer multi-year treatment proposals to chronically ill folks. Someone diagnosed with kidney disease for example might sign a 5-year, $200,000 (i.e. $40,000/year) contract with a kidney disease treatment hospital, with various escape clauses.[14] The carrier would agree to this as it knows the typical 5-year kidney disease treatment costs and figures it would spend that amount anyway. Since the $200,000 is partly the consumer's and partly the carrier's, the consumer will shop wisely before contracting. Remember that providers' prices and

outcomes are public information in a consumer-driven system. A Certified Health Advisor (see below) can help the consumer chose the best 5-year treatment option.

The consumer would chose the best 'value' over 5 years: a provider that offers the treatments he/she desires (transplant, dialysis, nutritional counseling, support groups, etc) at a competitive price.

The provider faces interesting economic incentives here. Depending on the specific kidney problems, the provider may recommend a kidney transplant in year 1. This represents an initial major expenditure, but allows the provider 4 years of low-cost treatment to recoup its investment, as the patient will be healthier post-transplant.

Alternatively, the provider may recommend years of dialysis and alternative treatments, attempting to improve the patient's health and save the transplant costs.

Ultimately, according to consumer-driven advocates, the choice is made by a combination of the policy holder, the Certified Health Advisor, the provider and the carrier.[15]

Different policies and different treatments for different people over different time periods. How can the poor consumer understand what to buy and how to navigate through the process? Proponents suggest that a new advisory industry will develop—Certified Healthcare Advisors. Much like Certified Financial Planners who help people negotiate the financial services industry maze, so Certified Healthcare Advisors will help people purchase and use their health insurance. CHAs will monitor costs and results and help clients negotiate with providers. In Herzlinger's proposed model, Certified Health Advisors will work under a new Healthcare Securities and Exchange Commission type authority. The Healthcare SEC would fulfill the following functions:

Private-sector analysis The Healthcare SEC should require public dissemination of all outcomes for providers, including clinical measures of quality and related costs. The Healthcare SEC would focus on outcomes, not processes or process compliance;

An independent agency with a singular focus The financial SEC is an independent agency charged solely with overseeing the integrity of security and the exchanges on which they are traded. The healthcare SEC should have a similar, singular focus;

Penalties The Healthcare SEC should have the power to penalize undercapitalized and unethical carriers and providers, including imprisonment, civil monetary penalties and refunds of illegal profits;

Private sector disclosure and auditing The new Healthcare SEC should delegate the power to derive measurements to an FASB-type organization.[16]

Many current medical providers claim that medicine is too complex for this type of measurement. Yet Herzlinger claims virtually every interest group that has been required to measure its outcomes claims its work is so diffuse that its impact cannot be measured.[17] The financial services industry opposed Roosevelt's establishment of the SEC—just a many entrenched healthcare interests oppose establishment of a Healthcare SEC.

Can all this happen? The answer depends in part on what American consumers demand, and in part on how the government proceeds.

The Government's Role. Consumer-driven healthcare proponents advocate less government involvement in healthcare: fewer mandates and fewer, though appropriate, regulations.

Dr. David Gratzer, for example, argues that state mandates boost health insurance premiums without much affect on outcomes. Mandated services, he argues, reflect the political power of healthcare provider lobbying groups at the state level.[18] Providers use their political power to protect their guild-like position. Gratzer notes that state mandated benefits have increased from 7 in 1965 to 1823 in 2004 with states such as New Jersey leading the way. Not surprisingly, New Jersey premiums are about triple those in Iowa.

Yet I was unable to find any data linking more state mandates to increased longevity or better health outcomes—after a Google search and a review of the US Statistical Abstract, the Kaiser Family Foundation website, the Iowa and New Jersey state websites and the National Center for Health Statistics website. State mandates exist in a non-competitive healthcare market where the political system allocates resources—regardless the medical need.

Consumer driven advocates want fewer healthcare mandates and less governmental regulation. Herzlinger explains why: 'The role of government is not to micromanage business…Rather, the role of government is to prevent fraud and abuse, help the needy, and provide transparency.'[19] These mandates and other government involvement in our healthcare inhibit, rather than assist, systemic improvement. She sees 3 roles for the government in a consumer-driven system:

1. Oversee the solvency and integrity of participants;
2. Provide transparency;
3. Provide subsidies for the needy.[20]

She advocates three main pieces of legislation to accomplish this.[21] **First,** she wants to break the link between employment and health insurance. Individuals, not employers, should choose their health coverage. This likely means merging the 'group' and 'non-group' markets and offering the same prices and tax benefits to individuals purchasing independently as those purchasing in a group.

What's Wrong with Employer Based Health Insurance?

Employer-based health coverage originated during WWII's war-based economy; it has no economic justification today. Your employer does not purchase your auto insurance, homeowners insurance, food or house—- why should he/she continue to purchase your health coverage? Your employer, after all, is expert at making, selling or servicing something. He/she is not knowledgeable about your medical needs or desires, nor expert at evaluating your personal healthcare options and designing an appropriate program.

Furthermore, your employer's health insurance purchase criteria differs from yours. Your employer wants reasonable coverage at low cost. He/she provides benefits to attract and retain employees, so wants coverage that is good enough to keep employees from leaving. Your employer gains little from providing better coverage, especially at a higher cost as this will negatively impact his/her financial health.

You, on the other hand, want excellence. If you're sick, you want the best care—not just 'good enough' care. But employer-based health coverage reduces your ability to choose and demand excellence from your carrier or providers. Both respond to your employer's purchasing decisions, not to yours.

Consumer advocates argue that employer based healthcare harms employees, employers, carriers and providers. It harms **employees** by restricting their healthcare options and reducing their consumer sovereignty. It harms **employers** by putting an unnecessary economic burden on them. It harms **carriers** by reducing their ability to provide high value, innovative products, rather than lowest cost products. It harms **providers** by reducing their ability to respond to consumer demands with innovation and long term value, and to differentiate themselves based on excellence or value.

Since neither carriers nor providers in an employer based healthcare system can respond to consumer demands for excellence, our entire healthcare system suffers.

Interestingly, the Massachusetts healthcare reform of 2006—one of the evolutionary legs of consumerism discussed Chapter 12—both supported and undermined this employment-health coverage link. The individual mandate and merger of group and non-group markets started to break the link, but the employer mandate served to solidify it. Perhaps this helps make Herzlinger's case: that the government should not try to micromanage healthcare through regulation.

Herzlinger's **second** proposed legislation requires transparency— that all providers and carriers to publish publicly available audited price and outcome statements, much like the SEC does with financial services companies.

Third, and far more complicated, she wants providers to adjust for risk. In other words, providers must be paid *more* for treating those who are sick than for treating those who are well or relatively healthier.[22] Risk adjustment ensures that providers and carriers are not motivated to avoid sick folks. This might be accomplished by eliminating all medical underwriting of insurance policies, making health insurance 'guaranteed issue' and using community rated premiums. Michael Cannon and Michael Tanner explain that with long-term insurance policies, beneficiaries could switch from plan to plan:

If the new plan would not accept the beneficiary's voucher as payment in full, then the old plan could be required to make a severance payment to the new plan...Because the beneficiary's decision to switch would require the former carrier to pay a competitor whatever that competitor demands, private carriers would be heavily discouraged from underserving sicker patients.

This could preserve the beneficiary's freedom of choice and lead to greater competition among carriers on the basis of price and quality.

Used in tandem, risk-adjusted vouchers and long-term contracts would give the government complementary tools to protect [beneficiaries] from adverse screening decisions by insurers.[23]

An individual mandate seems unnecessary. Wider differentiation of insurance products—i.e. market reform—alone may induce higher rates of coverage. States requiring auto insurance, for example, have about the same coverage rates as states that do not. The current impediment to full (or almost so) health insurance coverage nationally is less a legal issue than an economic one: current, heavily regulated health insurance policies cost too much for many to afford.

The Consumer's Role. Consumer-driven healthcare works when consumers actively participate—by demanding excellence and high value from carriers and providers, and by practicing good health management regimens. Good health management includes personal weight management, exercise and nutrition—the key good health factors noted by the Ontario Premier's Council on Health Strategy in Chapter 6. Under high-deductible consumer-driven healthcare plans, practicing these is not only good for your health but also for your pocket book.

Competitive shopping seems a commonly held value among Americans. We expect suppliers—of any product—to promote their products based on value: miles per gallon, resale value, comfort, ease of use, status or other. We are used to the consumer role.

But we are—today—not used to the 'good health management' role. This is partially because we are shielded from our true disease costs, claim consumer-driven advocates, given our current health insurance policy options. If Americans who do not exercise reasonably, eat appropriately or smoke are forced to pay more for their healthcare, then perhaps these (unhealthy) lifestyles will change.

Consider Clarian Health of Indiana with 13,000 employees.[24] Effective 2009, Clarian will introduce financial penalties for poor health—with plenty of caveats and employee protections, according to Human Resources Vice President Sheriee Ladd. Employees with a Body Mass Index above 30 will pay $10 extra for health insurance per paycheck, blood pressure above 140/90 will pay $5 extra, and blood glucose levels above 120 will also pay $5. Clarian's hope: by inducing employees to practice better health, they will, in fact, get healthier and company premiums will decrease.

Clarion's healthcare utilization rate has increased by double digits recently, due in part to poor employee health according to Ladd. Indiana ranks 4th nationally in obesity rates and second in incidence of smoking—both key drivers of Clarions' employee healthcare utilization rates. Clarion had already established voluntary good-health promotion programs for employees: free personal health coaches, fitness centers and nutritionist consultations. But healthcare utilization rates continued to increase, as did Clarion's premiums. Clarion hopes to reduce costs by attacking the behavioral forces driving utilization: obesity, smoking and lack of exercise.

Clarian and similar companies hope to add 'maintaining good health' to 'shopping wisely' as an American value. This is clearly an evolutionary step at its very early stages.

Advocates hope that shifting financial incentives to consumers for good health promotion will impact total US healthcare costs. Consider the impact of Blue Cross Blue Shield of Massachusetts' **Tips for Better Health**: [25]

1. Eat balanced meals for weight management. The US CDC estimates that excess body fat costs the US **$31 billion** annually for treatment of overweight people who develop heart disease;

2. Exercise daily. The CDC claims that direct medical costs associated with physical inactivity in 2000 exceeded **$75 billion**. Also if 10% of adults began a regular walking program we would save $5.6 billion in heart disease medical costs;

3. Quit smoking. Smoking costs **$68 billion** in direct and indirect costs annually;

4.   Chose generics whenever possible. The Blue Cross Blue Shield Association estimates a **$10 billion** potential annual saving by switching to generics.

Consumer-driven advocates hope that the savvy consumer will avoid smoking, eat well and exercise, and shop wisely for medical services.

Can this work? Maybe a tall order. Our land use patterns discourage daily exercise; our car ownership and usage patterns do also. Over the past 20 to 40 years, Americans have exercised less in their daily lives than Canadians or Europeans as discussed in Chapter 7. We commute longer, relax less and eat more poorly than others. Changing these trends—toward more daily exercise, better nutrition, less stress—looks ominously like 'transforming the nature of Americans.' Popper warned about this.

But if our thesis is correct—that some 1/3 of medical cost increases since 1990 are directly attributable to obesity—then perhaps good public policy calls for offering economic inducements to Americans to lose weight and manage their own health. Even Popper might agree that economic inducements are an appropriate social change mechanism.... not 'cost-shifting' as much as 'responsibility-shifting.' Paraphrasing Arnold Relman's defense of single payer systems (from Chapter 5) that 'in the long run nothing else is likely to work'—do we have any more reasonable options than inducing Americans to take better control of their own health? In the long run, will any other public policies likely achieve our desired goals of better health at lower prices?

Those able to accept this 'good health responsibility' get rewarded with lower medical costs / health insurance premiums; those unable, pay more. Consumer-driven advocates want the market to induce more personal healthcare responsibility among Americans—with, in Herzlinger's words, appropriate subsidies for the needy.

Consumer Driven Healthcare and our Six Systemic Features:

1.   **High Number of Uninsured:** A consumer-based system can insure everyone. Advocates anticipate that carriers will offer a broad range of products, including many low- or moderate cost plans. The government could offer subsidies for the needy/and or chronically ill;

2. **Medical Arms Race:** A consumer-based system would induce providers to respond to consumer demand with different treatment types unlike our current model where all general hospitals offer the same treatments;

3. **Moral Hazard:** A consumer-based system would not be a fee-for-service system, thus reducing providers' motivations to over-treat. Patients armed with price and outcome data could purchase the services they desire;

4. **Ineffective Chronic Disease Care and Prevention:** Long term insurance policies would induce providers and carriers to take a long term economic interest in their patients, unlike today;

5. **Uneven Treatment Quality Nationally:** Transparency would let the market equalize treatment quality. Consumer advocates assume that all providers would aim for outcome excellence rather than today's process compliance;

6. **Relatively Low Quality and Safety Investments:** Transparency, again, would induce quality improvements and safety investments. Providers would have an economic interest in providing high quality, safe treatments.

Note an interesting interaction among solutions to these problems. If consumer-based competition among providers actually eliminates the medical arms race, moral hazard and other systemic inefficiencies, then healthcare costs will fall. Remember Dartmouth Medical School researchers' estimate that up to 1/3 of American healthcare expenditures go to treatments that provide no discernable benefits. Reducing healthcare costs by 1/3 would radically reduce health insurance premiums, thus making insurance more affordable. Market forces would solve our uninsured problem.

At the same time, transparency would motivate providers toward excellence. Remember the Chapter 10's VHA lesson, as summarized by acting undersecretary Jonathan Perlin: quality is less expensive.

Consumer driven healthcare reduces costs and improves outcomes. Everyone wins…at least in theory.

***

The US healthcare market with its fee-for-service reimbursement model currently exhibits the six systemic failures discussed throughout this book. These blunt transparency and results-based competition. As we have already discussed, US providers currently compete on reputation or process compliance (guild like), rather than on price and results (market like). American hospitals and physician groups do not even offer price lists or engage in price competition for patients.

There is a medical system, however that <u>does</u> compete on price and outcomes: the international medical tourism business. Facilities in India, Thailand and Brazil for example, market to an international clientele including wealthy third-world nationals, uninsured Americans, and Britons and Canadians facing long waits for service.

Luring Americans, Britons, Canadians from their domestic providers is a hurdle for third world providers to overcome. India, for example, by reputation poor and dirty is not immediately an attractive destination for complex, life-threatening surgeries. Yet it competes aggressively for international patients. Let's look at the Escorts Heart Institute of New Delhi—a focused factory specializing in cardiac procedures—to see how.

Dr. Naresh Trehan established Escorts in 1988 after spending 20 years practicing in Manhattan and teaching at the New York University School of Medicine. Escorts specializes in cardiac surgery, interventional cardiology, pediatric cardiology and cardiac diagnostics. Its hospital has 325 beds, 9 operating rooms, 5 cath labs, 3 heart command centers, a 16 slice CT scan, MRI and a host of other facilities. It practices minimally invasive and robotic surgery. In-house laboratories perform a complete range of investigative tests in nuclear medicine, radiology, biochemistry, hematology, transfusion medicine and microbiology. It also has a blood bank.[26]

Since 1988 Escorts has performed more than 92,000 angiographies, 20,000 angioplasties and 50,000 cardiac surgical procedures. Patients call the facilities 'state of the art'[27] combining 'medical excellence with a human touch.'[28]

Escorts' international patients tend to be wealthy Asians and Middle Easterners who shop among hospitals worldwide. This level of competition forces Escorts to practice better customer service than a typical American general hospital. Escorts typically meets international patients at the airport, stocks their hospital room with fruits and drinks and offers options of private rooms, private chefs and dedicated staffs. Their fear: if they don't offer an outstanding consumer experience, they'll lose patients to their competitors.

Dr. Trehan claims that Escort's medical treatment success history has established its international credibility. 'We do over 4,000 heart operations a year and the mortality…is 0.8% which is even better than most places in the world. The other thing we measure is infection rate. Ours is 0.3% as compared to the world average of 1%.'[29]

Compare Escorts' 0.8% mortality to New York-Presbyterian Hospital's 4.7 mortality rate for heart value surgery or coronary artery bypass surgery from 2000—2003.[30] That's where former President Bill Clinton had his bypass surgery. Or Indianapolis' St. Vincent's Heart Center (post 2002-2004 medical arms race expenditure—see Chapter 4) mortality rate of 0.9%.[31] Or to Florida's Palm Beach Garden's Medical Center, where the state regulators found a 54% infection rate among a small sample of cardiac surgery patients in a spot survey (detailed in Chapter 9).

Why the better results? 'Our surgeons are much better' boasts Trehan.'[32] Escorts surgical teams practice more than typical American teams. They average over 60 heart bypass surgeries <u>per week</u>. Here's a comparison of Coronary Artery Bypass Graft surgeries annually by various hospitals. (This information was voluntarily submitted and is not comprehensive. Note that the Leapfrog Group recommends a 450 Coronary Artery Bypass Graft <u>minimum</u> rate per hospital per year [33]):

Facility	Annual Number of CABG Surgeries
Escorts	3214
Cleveland Clinic	1539
Massachusetts General Hospital, Boston	648
Duke University Hospital, Durham, NC	584
Emory University Hospital, Atlanta	417
St. Vincent Hospital, Indianapolis	344
Tufts-New England Medical Center, Boston	327
Mt Auburn Hospital, Cambridge, MA	168
Doctors Hospital Ohio Health, Columbus, OH	105
Capital Regional Medical Center, Tallahassee, FL	99
Aventure Hospital, Aventura, FL	96
St. Lukes Hospital, Duluth, MN	95
Huguley Memorial Medical Center, Dallas	95
Harris Methodist HEB, Bedford, Tx	84
Gottlieb Memorial, Melrose Park, IL	82
Menorah Medical Center, Overland Park, KS	80
Del Sol Medical Center, El Paso	78
Doctors Hospital, Dallas	77
Las Palmas Medical Center, El Paso	74
Aurora Sinai Medical Center, Milwaukee	67
Atlanta Medical Center, Atlanta	57
St Agnes Hospital, Fond Du Lac, WI	55
Highland Park Hospital, Highland Park, IL	49
Rose Medical Center, Denver	42
Sky Ridge Medical Center, Lone Tree, CO	22
Michael Reese Med Center, Chicago, IL	22

Interestingly, Escorts provides this information on its website: American hospitals typically do not, making comparison shopping much more difficult.

Escorts is a focused factory, unencumbered by DRG billing requirements or state procedural regulations. So Escorts, according to Dr. Trehan 'can take care of patients in a more comprehensive manner.'[34] It concentrates on excellence—much like McDonald's. If 'practice makes perfect' we can now understand Dr. Trehan's claim that Escort's surgeons are better than American.

Escort's price? Far less than American hospitals. Anecdotal evidence abounds of price savings at Escorts. Howard Staab, for example, a 53 year old carpenter from North Carolina faced up to a $200,000 estimated total cost for heart valve surgery and rehabilitation domestically in 2005. Lacking health insurance, his local hospital required a $50,000 deposit. The Escorts price: $10,000 including airfare, surgery and rehabilitation.[35]

Sixty-year old Carlo Gislimterti, a New Mexico restaurateur faced $120,000 in heart surgery costs domestically in 2005—but paid only $15,000 at Escorts. Jay Fink, a Sarasota businessman needed an artery stent, also in 2005. Estimated cost in Florida: between $130,000—$200,000. Escort price: $10,000.[36] It is unclear if these are typical savings.

International medical tourism is so price competitive that Escorts posts its price list on line.[37] The 8-page brochure lists both a la cart and package prices. Escorts accepts Mastercard and Visa. Some examples at the December, 2007 exchange rate of 40 rupees per US dollar: (Note that two round trip air tickets from Boston plus 1 week's stay for two in a business class New Delhi hotel costs about $3000—$3500.)

Procedures (a la carte)	Approximate Cost in US Dollars
CT Scan, head with pituitary fossa	$ 68
Chest X-ray, per view	$ 4
MRI, angiography of abdominal aorta	$125
Nuclear medicine: MUGA-Stress	$115
Cardiac services: ECG	$ 5
Cardiac services: PFT Dynamic	$ 25
Cath lab: EECP (per sitting)	$ 50
Room charges per day: single room	$182

Packages	Approximate Cost in US Dollars
Pace Maker: single chamber	$1225
(includes: 3 days in hospital – 1 in ICU and 2 in double room, routine blood tests, 1 ECG and 1 X-ray)	
R F Ablation	$1500
(includes hospitalization for 1 day in double room, routine blood tests, 1 ECG and 1 X-ray)	
Coronary angiography	$ 420
(includes hospitalization for 1 day, double room, routine blood tests, one ECG, one X-ray and 100 ml urograffin/omnipaque)	

With price and outcome data easily available, Escorts' competitors know how to compete—offer better outcomes at lower prices. Their (fairly obvious) strategy: hire better nurses and physicians, organize surgical teams more efficiently, offer more in-house training, purchase better equipment, provide better customer service and reduce the already low post-operative infection rate. Escorts will, of course, also improve. Through this competitive process, results-based competition can improve quality while reducing price. Just like other goods and services.

There is a second medical 'discovery mechanism' (Hayek's phrase) working here. Competitive pressures will likely motivate Escorts-type providers to innovate more quickly than process-controlled, highly regulated providers. Remember Michels' warning from Chapter 1 that administrators and bureaucrats gain power with codified regulations. Who's more likely to innovate—entrepreneurial, customer oriented Escorts, or a highly regulated, DRG dominated, bureaucratically controlled, horizontally integrated general hospital? Harvard's Herzlinger discusses innovation in non-regulated markets and suggests 'it is difficult to imagine that these results would have been obtained if the federal government had been limiting who could buy and sell these products, designing their characteristics, and…even specifying the budgets of the manufacturers.'[38]

Medicine is a young science, currently growing rapidly with technological breakthroughs and scientific discoveries. Guilds, on the other hand, are not innovators. They have economic incentives to restrict membership and slow innovation, and use codified rules and procedures to accomplish this. Guilds collapsed historically under the innovative power of entrepreneurs. Are American medical establishments today acting as guilds, with Escorts (and similar) innovating to threaten their status and power?

***

Consumer-driven advocates claim that increased healthcare regulation acts to promote the guild status of medical providers—and will produce poorer future healthcare results. Market competition, on the other hand, is the best mechanism to promote innovation, advance medical knowledge and improve the American healthcare delivery system.

Regina Herzlinger—the God Mother of Consumer Driven Healthcare—summarizes:

> A system controlled by the insurance companies or hospitals or government will kill us financially and medically—it will ruin our economy and deny us the healthcare services we need.[39]

Only consumers can save us.

CHAPTER 14
Healthcare Choices for America

Does consumer driven healthcare make sense? Can we quantify the results of all medical treatments—or just some? Can we validly extrapolate lessons from Escorts? Is the broad consumer driven theory based on too narrow a set of individual medical procedures such as heart bypass surgery—i.e. procedures with the easiest to obtain outcome data? Does consumer driven healthcare's quest for efficiency trample on systemic equity?

I don't know. I don't know if consumer driven theory will translate well into the real world of the US healthcare economy. It may—but we lack sufficient evidence for certainty.

<u>What to do?</u> This book is not an advocacy piece; it's an educational one. I aimed to outline the various healthcare options available to us and to evaluate them. When considering policy recommendations, I feel like Tevya, the milkman in *Fiddler on the Roof*:

On one hand, the Institute of Medicine calls for major changes in the US healthcare distribution system; on the other hand, none of the proposals discussed here provide a clear, absolute and compelling case for adoption;

On the first hand, our current healthcare system is bankrupting us; on the other hand, some of these proposals—an expanded Medicare, for example—may actually make our problems worse;

On the one hand, our current healthcare system does not provide consistent, high quality medical care for all Americans; on the other hand, none of these proposals are slam-dunks either;

On the one hand, single payer healthcare is a poor mechanism for fixing our healthcare mess; on the other hand, the mind-numbing, inefficient complexity of our current health insurance system is so overwhelming that single payer simplicity appears attractive;

On the one hand, our six systemic healthcare problems pose threats to the well-being of our population; on the other hand, the consumer driven solution—the only one that apparently address these problems—is untested in a large scale, real world environment.

This reminds me of an incident from my graduate days at Harvard. In class one day we discussed some theory or other designed to solve a major social problem. (I don't remember the theory or the problem.) In the face of student skepticism, the professor told this story:

A fellow walked through a secluded area, fell into a deep hole and shouted 'help, help'. Many hours later a lone passerby heard these cries and lowered the only thing available: a small branch. The fellow figured the branch would not support his weight and complained to the passerby who responded 'that's all I have.' The fellow then asked, 'Is anyone else up there?'

The proposals outlined in this book are—at their cores—'all we have.' There really isn't anyone else up there. We're faced with a healthcare mess that is destroying us and we have to do something—but all the options appear unappealing or risky.

Here's my suggested decision process: exclude the 'definite policy rejects' and then chose among the remaining potentials. From my analysis, single payer healthcare and a return to real managed care look like definite policy rejects. Adopting either will likely make our healthcare system <u>worse</u>.

That leaves the consumer driven option. Though apparently radical, I see four arguments in its favor.

First, it is not an obvious reject; it may work. It fits the Institute of Medicine's call for a sweeping design of the entire health system while honoring the American values of competition and individual responsibility. It follows from the current evolutionary trends evident in our healthcare system.

Second, it is incremental—Popper would approve. It keeps decisions in consumers' hands, not bureaucrats—Michels would approve. It promotes innovation through competition—Hayek would approve.

Third, it is low risk. We don't need to develop a huge new government program. We don't need to allocate new funds. We don't need to change hospital ownership from private to public or establish lots of new system rules. In fact, we don't need to do very much at all.

Fourth, it is not exclusive. Healthcare consumerism can exist alongside our current mish-mash of financing mechanisms. It may prove itself effective and become the dominant force in our future healthcare. Or it may fail. We don't know without more real world experience. But we don't need to bet the house on it.

So my policy recommendations: First, implement the proposals from Chapter 13:

1. Break the link between employment and healthcare coverage;
2. Promote transparency;
3. Adjust risk

Second, allow multi-year health insurance policies.

Third, allow consumers to purchase among 'comprehensive' policies that include all state mandated benefits, 'catastrophic' coverage that does not, and other policies that fall in between.

I don't know if these recommendations will solve the US healthcare problems. But they comply with the Institute of Medicine's call for a major healthcare system redesign and they're not obvious rejects.

And here's the dirty little secret: they're also the only viable and affordable option we have.

NOTES

Chapter 1: Orientation

[1] Karl R. Popper 'The Poverty of Historicism' Harper Torchbooks, 1957. See pages 64-70.
[2] Robert Michels, 'Political Parties' first published in English 1915
[3] Friederich Hayek, 'The Road to Serfdom' Routledge, 1937, condensed version at http://www.iea.org.uk/files/upld-publication43pdf?.pdf

Chapter 2: Systemic Values

[1] Jules B. Richmond and Rashi Fein, 'The Healthcare Mess' Harvard University Press, 2005, page 1
[2] The Economist 'Pocket World in Figures 2007' page 80
[3] Ibid. page 83

Chapter 3: Statistical Overview

[1] Figures from OECD Health Data, 2004
[2] Projection by Medicare, published in USA Today, 3/2/05
[3] This analysis comes from Phillip Longman, 'Best Care Anywhere: Why VA Healthcare is Better Than Yours' PoliPoint Press, 2007
[4] Economist World in Figures, 2004
[5] William, W Yu and Trena M. Ezzati-Rice, 'Medical Expenditure Panel Survey Statistical Brief #81', May 2005, Agency for Healthcare Research and Quality
[6] Benjamin Druss 'Comparing the National Economic Burden of Five Chronic Conditions' Health Affairs, vol. 20, no 6 (Nov-Dec 2001) pp. 233-241
[7] www.diabetes.org, data downloaded 9/21/07
[8] David Cutler 'The Value of Medical Spending in the United States, 1960-2000', New England Journal of Medicine, August 31, 2006, pp. 920 - 927

[9] Gerard Anderson, et. al. 'It's the Prices, Stupid: Why the United States is So Different from Other Countries', Health Affairs, Vol. 22, No3, May/June 2003

[10] 'Healthcare in America: Is More Better' Annals of Internal Medicine, Feb, 2003, report by Dartmouth Medical School researchers

[11] Institute of Medicine, 'Crossing the Quality Chasm', 2001

[12] National Committee on Quality Assurance, 2003

[13] The Economist 'Pocket World in Figures' 2007 edition, page 80

[14] OECD Data Book, 2006

[15] The Economist, op cit., page 83

Chapter 4: Six Healthcare Problems

[1] This discussion of Friedman comes from David Gratzer, 'The Cure' Encounter Books, 2006, page 34

[2] This is my own list; others label these differently. However, this is a fairly standard set of healthcare systemic problems, however labeled.

[3] Institute of Medicine, 'Care Without Coverage', May 2002

[4] J. Robinson and H. Luft, 'The Impact of Hospital Market Structure on Patient Volume, Average length of Stay and the Cost of Care,' Journal of Health Economics 4 (1985): 333-56

[5] David Dranove, 'The Economic Evolution of American Healthcare', Princeton University Press, 2000 page 47

[6] This example comes from Maggie Mahar, 'Money-Driven Medicine', Collins, 2006, pp. 40-42

[7] Boston Globe 'Scares Grow as Cancer Screening Rises' September 30, 2007, pages A 1, A 20

[8] Milton Roemer, 'Bed Supply and Hospital Utilization: A Natural Experiment', Hospitals, 35 (1961)
There is an alternative explanation. In 1957 and earlier, physicians could have been providing inferior care – a situation that the 1958 hospital expansion cured. This seems statistically unlikely, however, as the 1957 hospital bed utilization rate averaged only about 78%.

[9] Elliott S. Fisher, 'HealthCare in America: Is More Better?' Annals of Internal Medicine, February 2003. Fisher and colleagues compared regional Medicare spending difference and health outcomes. They found that while Medicare recipients living in high spending areas had more

physician visits, more tests and more hospitalizations, they showed no evidence of lower death rates or better health status.

[10] 'When Geography Influences Treatment Options', Washington Post, July 24, 2005, p A12, based largely on work of Dartmouth Medical School researchers. All quotes and references in this section come from this article.

[11] Phillip Longman, 'Best Care Anywhere: Why VA Healthcare is Better Than Yours' PoliPoint Press, 2007, page 82

[12] Kaiser Family Foundation 'Trends and Indicators in the Changing Health Care Marketplace' www.KFF.org

[13] Data from 'FFY 2002 Hospital Medicare Profit/Loss' Data Advantage Corporation, 304 West Liberty, Suite 400, Louisville, Kentucky

[14] Ranch Kimball, 'The Chronic Cost of Chronic Disease' Boston Globe 10/18/2007, page A13

[15] Professor Kenneth Thorpe of Emory University, Presentation to the Massachusetts Healthcare Council, Marlborough, Massachusetts March 13, 2007. This paragraph is based on that lecture.

[16] This case study comes from Ian Urbina 'In the Treatment of Diabetes, Success Often Does Not Pay', New York Times, January 11, 2006. All quotes from that article.

[17] Boston Globe, October 22, 2007, pages C1-C2

[18] Donald M Berwick and Sachin H. Jain 'Systems and Results: The Basis for Quality Care in Prepaid Group Practice' in Alain Enthoven and Laura Tollen, eds. 'Toward a 21st Century Health System' Jossey-Bass, 2004, page 27

[19] Jonathan Shaw, 'The Deadliest Sin' Harvard Magazine, March-April 2004, page 36

[20] J. Wennberg, J. Freeman and W. Culp 'Are Hospital Services Rationed in New Haven or Over-Utilized in Boston', Lancet 1(1987):1185:88

[21] This and the following points are discussed in Phillip Longman 'Best Care Anywhere' PoliPoint Press, 2007, pages 84 - 87

[22] Jonathan Skinner, John E. Wennberg 'How Much is Enough? Efficiency and Medicare Spending in the Last Six Month of Life' NBER Working Paper 6513, 1998.

[23] Elliot S. Fisher, 'More Medicine Is Not Better Medicine' New York Times, Dec 1, 2003, page A25

[24] Longman, page 86

[25] Elliot Fischer et al 'The Implications of Regional Variations in Medicare Spending, Part 2: Health Outcomes and Satisfaction with Care' Annals of Internal Medicine 138, no 4 (Feb 18, 2003) pages 288 - 298

[26] For more detail on systemic cost and quality controls, see Gary Fradin 'Moral Hazard in American Healthcare,' chapters 2 and 3

[27] IOM website

[28] Crossing the Quality Chasm, Institute of Medicine, March 2001

[29] To Err is Human, Institute of Medicine, 1999

[30] Centers for Disease Control and Prevention, 'Morbidity and Mortality Weekly Report 2000';49:149-53

[31] RAND Corporation, First National Report Card on Quality in Health Care in America, page 4.

[32] Longman, page 8

[33] Steve Lohr, 'Who Pays for Efficiency?' New York Times Jun 11, 2007

[34] This example comes from Longman, p. 66

[35] Preventing Medication Errors, Institute of Medicine, 2007

[36] N, Gibbs, A. Bower 'What Scares Doctors?' TIME, May 1, 2006 reported in Longman, page 87

[37] Richard Lord and Dr. Marylou Buyse, 'We pay for medical errors', Boston Globe, 9/12/2007, page A19

[38] Jeffrey Krasner 'Hospital aims to eliminate mistakes' Boston Globe, January 17, 2008, page D1

[39] See Chapter 10 on the Veteran's Administration Healthcare System for more detail.

Chapter 5: Pro-Single Payer Arguments

[1] www.pnhp.org. This information was downloaded 5/7/07

[2] http://www.pnhp.org/facts/angellintro.pdf

[6] http://pnhp.org/physiciansproposal/proposal/Physicians%20ProposalJAMA.pdf

[7] Executive Summary of the Proposal of the Physician's Working Group for Single-Payer National Health Insurance. Next quote from same source

[8] Julius B. Richmond and Rashi Fein 'The Health Care Mess' Harvard University Press, 2005, page 243

[9] Marcia Angell, et al of the Physicians' Working Group on Single Payer

National Health Insurance 'Proposal for Health Care Reform' Presentation to the Congressional Black Caucus, May 1, 2001

[10] John C. Goodman, Gerald L. Musgrave and Devon M. Herrick 'Lives at Risk' Rowman & Littlefield, 2004, page 9

[11] ibid., page 28. For years the British National Health Service imposed geographic restrictions on consumers.

[12] See Chapter 8 of this book for details

[13] Goodman, op cit. pages 28 - 29

[14] See Statistics Canada, www40.statcan.ca

[15] David Gratzer, Better Medicine, ECW Press, page 98

[16] Henry Aaron and William Schwartz with Melissa Cox 'Can We Say No?' Brookings Institution Press, 2005, page 25

[17] Dr. Michael Gordon, private communication

[18] Gratzer, op cit. page 54.

[19] These are anecdotal stories that I have either experienced in 2007 or heard from my clients.

[20] Jonathan Skinner, John E. Wennber 'How Much is Enough? Efficiency and Medicare Spending in the Last Six Months of Life' NBER Working Paper 6513, 1998

[21] National Committee on Quality Assurance, 2004 Quality Report

[22] ibid.

[23] Quoted in Regina Herzlinger, Market Driven Healthcare' Perseus Books, 1997, page 77

[24] Pat Armstrong and Hugh Armstrong, 'Wasting Away: The Undermining of Canadian Health Care' Oxford University Press, 2003, page176

[25] NCQA, op cit.

[26] ibid.

[27] American Academy of Actuaries 'Issue Brief on Pay for Performance' October 2005

[28] This section relies on Michael Porter and Elizabeth Olmsted Teisberg, 'Redefining Health Care' Harvard Business School Press, 2006, pages 86 – 88. References to cystic fibrosis comes from http://www.newyorker.com/archive/2004/12/06/041206fa_fact?currentPage=8

[29] Sherwin B. Nuland, 'Medical Fads: Bran, Midwives and Leeches,' New York Times, June 25, 1995, section 4, p 16

[30] Arnold S. Relman 'Medicine and the Free Market: The Health of Nations' New Republic, March 7, 2005. Much of Relman's position relies

on work by economist Kenneth Arrow. All quotes are from this article unless otherwise noted

[31] Arnold S. Relman 'A Second Opinion' The Century Foundation, 2007. See Chapters 5 and 6.

[32] ibid. page 129

[33] ibid. page 130

[34] Relman does not make this intellectual leap. These are my interpretations

[35] For more on this and effects, see my Moral Hazard in American Healthcare, chapter 1.

[36] Phillip Longman, 'Best Care Anywhere: Why VA Health Care is Better than Yours' PoliPoint Press 2007

[36] Much more on this in Chapter 10

Chapter 6: Anti-Single Payer Arguments

[1] National Forum on Health, 'Canada Health Action: Building on the Legacy' vol. 1, Final Report: Ottawa, Minister of Public Works and Government Services, 1997, page 15.

[2] Ontario Premier's Council on Health Strategy 'Nurturing Health: A Framework on the Determinants of Health', Toronto, 1991 as summarized in Pat Armstrong and Hugh Armstrong 'Wasting Away' Oxford University Press, second edition, 2003, pages 13-16

[3] Richmond and Fein, page 92

[4] Pat Armstrong and Hugh Armstrong, 'Wasting Away: The Undermining of Canadian Health Care", Oxford University Press, 2003, page 43

[5] John C. Goodman, et. al. 'Lives at Risk', page 9

[6] Paul McDonald et al 'Waiting Lists and Waiting Times for Healthcare in Canada' Health Canada, Summary Report, July 1998)

[7] Goodman, page 9

[8] Relman, 'Second Opinion' page 148

[9] Nadeem Esmail and Michael Walker 'Waiting Your Turn: Hospital Waiting Lists in Canada, 13th edition', Fraser Institute, Critical Issues Bulletin, October 2003

[10] Sir John Bourn, comptroller and Auditor General, 'Inappropriate Adjustments to NHS Waiting Lists' UK National Audit Office, December 19, 2001

[11] Anthony Browne, 'Cash-Strapped NHS Hospitals Chase Private Patient Bonanza', The Observer, December 16, 2001

[12] Noelle O'Rourke and R. Edwards, 'Lung Cancer Treatment Waiting Times and Tumor Growth' Clinical Oncology (Royal College of Radiologists) 12, no 3 (June 2000): 141-144

[13] Audit Commission 'Waiting for Elective Admission', Health: Acute Hospital Portfolio (London, Audit Commission, June 2003)

[14] Audit Commission 'Waiting for Elective Admission', Health: Acute Hospital Portfolio (London, Audit Commission, June 2003)

[15] Cathy Schoen et al 'Comparison of Health Care Systems:' Commonwealth Fund, Issue Brief, May, 2002

[16] Goodman, page 10

[17] RAND Health Insurance Experiment on rand.org/health/projects/ hie. See in particular 'Research Highlights: The Health Insurance Experiment: A Classic RAND Study Speaks to the Current Healthcare Reform Debate.'

[18] Goodman, page 9

[19] Data from OECD Health Data Book, 2002. Same source for CT scanner chart.

[20] Tom Arnold, 'X-Ray Labs Dangerously Outdated' National Post, October 12, 2000. Mr. Arnold uses data supplied by the Canadian Association of Radiologists

[21] David Green and Laura Casper Delay, 'Denial and dilution: The Impact of NHS Rationing on Heart Disease and Cancer', London: Institute of Economic Affairs, 2000

[22] Gerald F. Anderson and Peter S. Hussey, 'Multinational Comparisons of Health Systems Data' Commonwealth Fund, October 2000

[23] Goodman, page 18

[24] Michael Porter and Elizabeth Olmsted Teisberg, 'Redefining Health Care' Harvard Business School Press, 2006, page 89

[26] Angell simply wants a national Medicare-type operation. Relman attempts to outline a national provider scheme in 'A Second Opinion', chapter 5. His scheme is artificial and would be imposed on providers – another example of top-down, utopian engineering which can never work: far too many variables and moving parts to codify and define a priori.

[27] Heralinger, 'Consumer Driven Healthcare', page 130

[28] Herzlinger, 'Who Killed Healthcare' p. 61
[29] Porter, op cit. page 39

Chapter 7: Canadian medicare

[1] J.K. Inglehart, 'Restoring the Status of an Icon' Health Affairs, May/June 2000, page 137
[2] OECD Databook, 2004
[3] Economist Pocket World in Figures, 2007.
[4] Canada's Healthcare System, 2005 edition, published by authority of the Minister of Health
[5] Ibid., page 5. Descriptions of the Five Basic Principals are direct quotes.
[6] Ibid.
[7] Ibid., page 7
[8] David Gratzer, editor, 'Better Medicine: Reforming Canadian Healthcare' ECW Press, 2002, page 37
[9] James Travers, 'Don't Expect Prescription for User Fees' Toronto Star, June 28, 2001, A27
[10] CBC News, March 20, 2005
[11] CBC News, op cit.
[12] Ibid.
[13] This discussion comes from John Pucher and Ralph Buechler, 'Why Canadians Cycle More Than Americans' Transportation Policy 13 (2006) 265-279. All quotes and references in this section come from this article unless otherwise indicated.
[14] Population figures Googled January, 2008; McDonald's franchise figures from http://www.entrepreneur.com/franchises/mcdonalds/282570-0.html
[15] Craig C.L., Russell S.J., Cameron C. and Bauman A., 'Twenty-year trends in physical activity among Canadian adults' Canadian Journal of Public Health 2004;95(1):59-63
[16] http://www.thecanadianencyclopedia.com/index.cfm?PgNm=TCE&Params=M1ARTM0012163
[17] M. Walker and G. Wilson, 'Waiting Your Turn: Hospital Waiting Lists in Canada' (Vancouver: The Frasier Institute, 2000) page 37
[18] Dr. Albert Schumacher, President of the Ontario Medical Association,

'A Prescription for Health Care Reform' address to the Canada Club, Toronto, March 19, 2001, reported in Gratzer, op. cit.

[19] OECD data reported in Gratzer, op cit.

[20] L. Priest, 'Doctors are Told to Warn Patients of Faulty Tests', Toronto Globe and Mail, March 19, 2001, page A1

[21] Cathy Schoen, et. al. 'Comparison of Health Care System Views and Experience in Five Nations, 2001' Commonwealth Fund Issue Brief, 2002

[22] CBC, 'Waiting List Report Care', November 2006

[23] Gratzer, op cit. page 17

[24] CBC News on-line, June 10, 2005. All quotes in this section from this source.

[25] Wall Street Journal, June 13, 2005

Chapter 8: British National Health Service

[1] Much of this chapter relies on 'Can We Say No?' by Henry J. Aaron and William B. Schwartz with Melissa Cox, Brookings Institution Press, 2005. A version of this chapter appeared in my 'Moral Hazard in American Healthcare,' 2007

[2] Aaron ibid., pages 38 - 39

[3] Anthony Browne and Matthew Young, 'NHS Reform – Towards Consensus?' The Observer, April 17, 2002

[4] Aaron, op cit, page 20

[5] 'Waiting List Figures, November 2001' UK Department of Health, Statistical Press Release, January 11, 2002

[6] Michael White and John Carvel, 'Private Ops Offer to Cut NHS Queue' The Guardian, December 6, 2001

[7] Matthew Young and Eamonn Butler, 'The Million-Year Wait' Adam Smith Institute, 2002

[8] This paragraph comes from John C. Goodman, Gerlad L. Musgrave and Devon M. Herrick 'Lives at Risk' Rowan and Littlefield, 2004

[9] Another reason for purchasing private health insurance: to see your physician of choice. My thanks to Dr. Michael Gordon for this input. Personal correspondence.

[10] Caroline Richmond, Canadian Medical Association Journal, 1996; 154:378-381

[11] Aaron, page 25

[12] ibid., page 161

[13] ibid. page 26

[14] Goodman, page 28

[15] ibid., pages 29 - 30

[16] statistics.gov.uk

[17] Arnold Kemp 'Ten Years of Ignoring Suffering' The Observer, December 9, 2001

[18] Aaron, Chapter 5. Much of this section relies on Aaron's analysis.

[19] HM Treasury, Chancellor of the Exchequer's Budget Statement, Speech March 16, 2005

[20] Much of this section relies on Aaron, Chapter 3

[21] This estimate comes from the Guardian, February 13, 2003 'Victory for Haemophilia Patients'

[22] This is Aaron's conclusion

[23] For example, see James Meikle, The Guardian, February 13, 2003 'Victory for Haemophilia Patients'. Some 4000 British hemophiliacs had received blood tainted with HIV or hepatitis. The British Government 'sought to end a long-running dispute with the haemophilia community by finally putting all British patients on the same footing over access to synthetic clotting factor known as recombinant.' This governmental decision will cost approximately $125 million over 3 years.

[25] James Meikle 'Donor Hunt to Ease Kidney Shortge' Guardian, May 31, 2005

[26] Aaron, page 44

Chapter 9: US Medicare

[1] David A. Hyman, 'Medicare Meets Mephistopheles' CATO Institute, 2006

[2] Medicare Disbursements by Type of Beneficiary: 1990 to 2005 on cms. hhs.gov/ReportsTrustFunds/, downloaded 10/1/2007

[3] Medicare Enrollees: 1980 – 2005. Source US Centers for Medicare and Medicaid Services, cms.hhs.gov/researchers

[4] Gilbert M. Gaul, 'Early Deals set the Stage for Today's Problems' Washington Post July 24, 2005 page A 12

[5] Thomas Healey, Senior Fellow at Harvard's Kennedy School of Government, Boston Globe June 9, 2007, page A11. Emphasis my own.

[6] US General Accounting Office 'High Risk Series: An Update (Repeat Nos. 03-119) 2003 gao.gov/pas/2003/d03119.pdf

[7] Gilbert Gaul, 'Bad Practices Net Hospitals More Money' Washington Post, July 24, 2003, page A1. Gaul writes that for every $1000 that Medicare pays to providers, it invests just $1 or $2 to oversee and improve patient care.

[8] Richard A. Epstein, forward to David A Hyman 'Medicare Meets Mephistopheles' CATO Institute, 2006 page xii

[9] Jerry Kruse, 'Saving Medicare' Annals of Family Medicine May 2006 pages 274-275

[10] Michael Porter, MIT Health Information Technology Symposium 7/19/2006 www.icvclients.com

[11] Jonathan Skinner, Elliott S. Fisher and John E. Wennberg, 'The Efficiency of Medicare' Working Paper 8395, National Bureau of Economic Research, July 2001

[12] Jonathan Skinner, John E. Wennberg 'How Much is Enough?' NBER Working Paper 6513, 1998

[13] ibid.

[14] Wennberg's analysis comes from Maggie Mahar 'Money-Driven Medicine' Collins, 2006 page 172

[15] Gilbert Gaul, op cit.

[16] Gina Kolata 'Patients in Florida are Lining Up for All That Medicare Covers' New York Times, September 13, 2003, page A1. Following quotes from that article.

[17] Marilyn Moom and Christina Boccuti 'Location, Location, Location; Geographic Spending Issues and Medicare Policy' Urban Institute, June 21, 2002, quoted in Hyman, page 50

[18] Elliot S. Fisher et al 'The Implication of Regional Variations in Medicare Spending Part 2' Annals of Internal Medicine 138 (2003): page 288

[19] Katherine Baicker and Amitabh Chandra 'Medicare Spending, the Physician Workforce, and Beneficiaries' Quality of Care' Health Affairs Web Exclusive, April 7, 2004 quoted in Hyman, op. cit. page 25

[20] Information in this section, including the discussion of QIOs and State Regulators and case study of Palm Beach Gardens Medical Center, comes from the Washington Post analysis of Medicare that ran July 24 – 26, 2005.

[21] Hyman, page 54

[22] Hyman, page 28

[23] Bruce Vladeck 'The Political Economy of Medicare' Health Affairs 19 (1999): page 22

[24] Hyman, page 31

[25] Much of this section comes from Regina Herzlinger 'Who Killed Healthcare' McGraw-Hill, 2007 Chapter 5, including information about DaVita, Amgen and hematocrit issues.

[26] Time Magazine, 'The Price of Life' January 1, 1973

[27] Herzlinger, page 116

[28] ibid., page 117

[29] ibid. page 118

[30] idid., page 123

[31] ibid. page 119. Herzlinger refers to Tom Hamburger and Walter F. Roche Jr 'Congress Closes with a Pork-filled Flourish; Dialysis Industry, Other Intrests that Donated to Lawmakers Get Lavish End-of-Session Breaks' Los Angeles Times, December 21, 2006, Part A, page 1

[32] ibid. page 123

[33] Ibid., page 123. Herzlinger refers to Dennis Cotter, et al, 'Translating Epoetin Research into Practice' Health Affairs, vol. 25, no 5 (September-October 2006) pages 1249-1260

[34] Dennis Cotter 'Translating Epoetin Research into Practice' Health Affairs, vol. 25, no 5 quoted in Herzlinger, ibid. page 123

[35] ibid., page 126

[36] These results from Herzlinger, ibid., page 121

[37] Gaul, 'Early Deals Set the Stage for Today's Problems' Washington Post, July 24, 2005 page A12

[38] Ibid.

[39] 2006 Annual Report of the Board of Trestees of the Federal Hospital Insurance and Federal Supplementary Medical Insurance Trust Funds, page 3. Emphasis my own.

[40] Status of the Social Security and Medicare Programs: A Summary of the 2007 Annual Reports. ssa.gov/OACT/TRSUM/trsummary.html

[41] Health forum, AHA Annual Survey Data, 2000-2005, in American Hospital Association 'Underpayment by Medicare and Medicaid Fact Sheet' October 2006

[42] Margaretann Cross 'Confronting the Medicare Cost Shift' Managed Care, December 2006

[43] This calculation: The American Hospital Association reports that 2004 Medicare hospital underpayments were $15 billion (67%) and Medicaid underpayments were $7.1 billion (33%). I multiplied the Medicare portion times the total estimated family contribution.

[44] Michael F. Cannon and Michael D. Tanner 'Healthy Competition' CATO Institute, 2005, page 84

[45] Jonathan Skinner and John E. Wennberg ' Perspective: Exceptionalism or Extravagance? What's the Difference About Healthcare in South Florida?' Web exclusive, Health Affairs, August 13, 2003, quoted in Maggie Mahar 'Money Driven Medicine' Collins, 2006, page 168.

[46] David Cutler 'The Value of Medical Spending in the United States 1960 – 2000' New England Journal of Medicine 2006;355(9):920-927

Chapter 10: Veterans Administration Healthcare

[1] Much of the data and discussion in this chapter comes from Phillip Longman 'Best Care Anywhere', PoliPointPress, 2007 and Phillip Longman, 'The Best Care Anywhere', Washington Monthly, January/February 2005.

[2] New England Journal of Medicine, May 29, 2003 'Effect of the Transformation of the Veterans Affairs Healthcare System on the Quality of Care'. This and footnotes 3 – 7 appear in Longmans's book and / or article.

[3] Annals of Internal Medicine, 2004; 141(4):242-281

[4] Annals of Internal Medicine, 2004, 141(12):928-945

[5] 'Risk adjusted mortality as an indicator of outcomes: comparison of the Medicare Advantage Program with the Veterans' Health Administration' Managed Care 2006; 44(4):359-365

[6] Longman, page 3

[7] Department of Veterans Affairs 'Performance and Accountability Report' FY 2005

[8] Sheila Weatherill 'The VHA's Commitment to Accountability: A 'Third Way' for Medicare?' HealthcarePapers, Vol. 5, No 4, 2005:38-42

[9] Matthew W. Morgan 'The VA Advantage: The Gold Standard in Clinical Informatics' HealthcarePapers, Vol. 5, no 4, 2005:26-29

[10] Nancy J. Wilson and Kenneth W. Kizer 'The VA Healthcare System: An Unrecognized National Safety Net' Health Affairs, Vol. 16, No 4

[11] Longman, page 6
[11] Gilbert Gaul 'Revamped Veteran's Health Care Now a Model' Washington Post August 22, 2005 page A01
[12] 'The Best Medical Care in the US' BusinessWeek July 17, 2006
[13] Wilson and Kizer, op cit
[14] Longman, pages 22 - 23
[15] Longman, page 32
[16] Quoted in Longman, page 36
[17] Gaul, op cit
[18] Longman, page 38
[19] BusinessWeek
[20] Longman, page 40.
[21] BusinessWeek, op cit
[22] BusinessWeek, op cit
[23] Longman, Washington Monthly
[24] Gaul, op cit
[25] Longman, page 75
[26] Brown, SH et al 'International Journal of Medical Informatics, 2003 69:135-156, referenced in Longman, page 76
[27] Longman Washington Monthly
[28] Longman, page 76
[29] Longman, Washington Monthly
[30] Longman, page 55
[31] BusinessWeek, op cit
[32] Longman, page 110
[33] Gaul, op cit
[34] BusinessWeek, op cit

Chapter 11: Managed Care

[1] Alain Enthoven 'The History and Principles of Managed Competition' Health Affairs Supplement, 1993, page 27
[2] ibid., page 29
[3] Alain C. Enthoven and Laura A. Tollen, editors 'Toward a 21st Century Health System' Jossey-Bass, 2004, page xxix
[4] David Dranove, The Economic Evolution of American Healthcare, Princeton University Press, 2000, page 40

[5] ibid., page 39

[6] Much of this analysis is based on Regina Herzlinger, Who Killed Healthcare, McGraw-Hill, 2007, pages 36 - 46

[7] ibid., page 43

[9] ibid., page 47

[8] ibid., page 43

[10] Jan Gregoire Coombs, 'The Rise and Fall of HMOs' University of Wisconsin Press, 2005, page 56

[11] Dranove, op cit. page viii

[12] ibid. page 25

[13] ibid. page 58

[14] ibid. page x

[15] CBO Testimony: Statement of Robert d. Reischauer, Deputy Director, Congressional Budget Office before the Subcommittee on Oversight, Committee on Ways and Means, US House of Representatives, June 27, 1979

[16] Dranove, op. cit. pages 78 - 79

[17] J. Wennberg, et. al. 'Are Hospital Services Rationed in New Haven or Over-Utilized in Boston?' Lancet 1 (1987): 1185-1188

[18] See also Dartmouth Atlas of Healthcare, Jack Wennberg, ed (Chicago: American Publishing, 1996, 1999) which shows variation in a wide range of treatments diagnostic tests and drug therapies.

[19] T. Wickizer et. al. 'Does Utilization Review Reduce Unnecessary Hospital Care and Contain Costs?' Medical Care 27 (1989): 632-47

[20] V. G. Freeman et. al 'Lying for Patients: Physician Deception of Third Party Payers', Archives of Internal Medicine (1999): 2263 - 70

[21] Sean Hennessy et. al 'Retrospective Drug Utilization Review, Prescribing Errors and Clinical Outcomes' Journal of the American Medical Association, Vol. 290, No. 11, September 17, 2003

[22] Stephen Rosenberg, et. al. 'Effect of Utilization Review in a Fee-for-Service Health Insurance Plan' New England Journal of Medicine, Volume 333: 1326-31, November 16, 1995

[23] Norman Kalant et.al. 'How Valid are Utilization Review Tools in Assessing Appropriate Care of Acute Care Beds' CMAJ June 27, 2000: 162(13)

[24] Dranove, op cit., page 84

[25] Herzlinger, Who Killed, page 48

[26] Economist, 2004

[27] Alain C. Enthoven 'The History and Principles of Managed Competition' Health Affairs Supplement, 1993; 'Why Managed Care Has Failed to Contain Health Costs' Health Affairs, Fall 1993. Quotes in this section come from these two articles unless otherwise indicated.

[28] Novalis Corporation 'American Values and Health Care Reform' Medical Benefits, march 30, 1993, page 7, reported in Regina Herzlinger 'Market Driven Healthcare' Perseus Books, 1997, page 51

[29] Stephen M Shortell and Julie Schmittdiel 'Prepaid Groups and Organized Delivery Systems: Promise, Performance, and Potential' in Enthoven and Tollen, editors, 'Toward a 21st Century Health System' John Wiley & Sons, 2004

[30] Herzlinger, Who Killed, page 47

[31] ibid., page 48

[32] Enthoven and Tollen, eds., op cit. Preface, page xxxi

[33] Regina Herzlinger 'Market Driven Healthcare' op cit. page 148

[34] Enthoven and Tollen, op cit. page xxxi

[35] Stephen M Shortell, op cit. page 14

[36] Dranove, op cit. Introduction

[37] Shortell and Schmittdiel, op cit. page 15

[38] ibid., page 19

[39] Arnold S. Relman 'Medicine and the Free Market: The Health of Nations' New Republic, March 7, 2005

Chapter 12: The Consumerism Trend

[1] http://www.census.gov/compendia/statab/tables/07s0144.xls

[2] These percentages come from our own internal sales data drawn from over 7,000 Harvard Pilgrim policies during the comparative years.

[3] The IRS allows variations on the basic high deductible plan. Some plans call for 100% coverage for covered services after deductible for in-network providers but less for out-of-network providers. Other plans call for less than 100% coverage from in-network providers up to some specified amount. All approved plans include pharmacy copayments even after the deductible has been reached.

[4] http://www.heritage.org/Research/HealthCare/wm1035.cfm

[5] http://content.nejm.org/cgi/content/full/354/20/2095

[6]   http://www.washingtonpost.com/wp-dyn/content/article/2007/03/04/AR2007030400227.html

[7]   http://www.businessweek.com/investor/content/apr2006/pi20060404_152510.htm

[8] http://content.nejm.org/cgi/content/full/354/20/2093

[9] This is very highly regulated and complicated. Depending on income, employment status and other factors, people could choose Commonwealth Care, Commonwealth Choice or traditional commercial coverage. I have tried in this section to focus on the values underlying Massachusetts's healthcare reform rather on underwriting or regulatory issues.

[10] Michael E. Porter and Elizabeth Olmsted Teisberg, 'Redefining Health Care' Harvard Business School Press, 200 6

[11] Regina Herzlinger, 'Who Killed Healthcare', McGraw-Hill, 2007

[12]   http://www.wbur.org/weblogs/commonhealth/wp-content/uploads/2007/10/murrays-speech.pdf

Chapter 13: Consumer Driven Healthcare

[1] 'Are Consumers the Cure for Broken Health Insurance' Harvard Business School Working Knowledge for Business Leaders, August 5, 2002, page 2. Quotes and references in the next 2 paragraphs come from this article.

[2] Healthcare Heretic, Economist, May 31, 2007

[3] ibid.

[4] ibid.

[5] Sean Silverthorne, 'Is Healthcare Making You Better – or Dead' HBS Working Knowledge, June 4, 2007 hbswk.hbs.edu

[6] Herzlinger 'Who Killed Healthcare' page 205

[7] Regina Herzlinger 'Market Driven Healthcare' pages 163 – 4, referring to work of Wickham Skinner, 'The Focused Factory' Harvard Business Review, May-June 1974, pages 113-122. I added the last clause of item #4.

[8] Herzlinger, Market Driven, page 179 - 180. Emphasis in original

[9] Gerald B. Healy, M.D. 'Ending medical errors with airline industry's help', Boston Globe, January 8, 2008, page A15

[10] Regina Herzlinger, 'Who Killed Healthcare' page 188

[11] Data in this paragraph comes from Time Magazine, Special Advertising Section 'America's Diabetes Epidemic' Nov 13, 2006

[12] Health Insurance Association of America, Sourcebook of Health Insurance Data - 1993

[13] Many of these ideas come from Herzlinger, Who Killed Healthcare, pages 175 - 179

[14] This example comes from Herzlinger, Who Killed Healthcare, pages 158 - 161

[15] ibid., page 160

[16] See Herzlinger, 'Who Killed Healthcare' pages 234 – 238 for more on the SEC and her proposed healthcare transparency model.

[17] ibid, page 234

[18] Dr. David Gratzer, 'The Cure' Encounter Books, 2006, pages 94 - 97

[19] Herzlinger 'Who Killed Healthcare' page 225

[20] ibid. page 214

[21] ibid. pages 163 - 166

[22] ibid, page 164. Emphasis in original.

[23] Michael F. Cannon and Michael D. Tanner 'Healthy Competition' CATO Institute, 2005, page 88

[24] WBUR Radio, 'Here and Now', August 14, 2007

[25] Blue Cross Blue Shield of Massachusetts 'Choices' consumer magazine, winter, 2003

[26] indicure.com/escorts_hearts_hospitals.html downloaded Nov 19, 2007

[27] John Lancaster 'Surgeries, Side Trips for Medical Tourists' Washington Post Foreign Service, October 21, 2004, page A1

[28] Subhash Vohra, 'Medical Tourism: American Find Low-Cost Treatment in India' Voice of America March 18, 2005

[29] ibid.

[30] Bloomberg News, January 27, 2005 'Indian Hospitals Lure Foreigners with $6,700 Heart Surgery'

[31] St. Vincent Heart Center website www.theheartcenter.com

[32] Washington Post, op. cit.

[33] http://www.ehirc.com/individuals/surgery_category_chart.html for Escorts (2005 data) and the Leapfrog Group website leapfroggroup.com for the others. Data downloaded on November 26, 2007

[34] Voice of America, op. cit.

[35] Washington Post, op. cit.

[36] Both examples from Jim Landers 'India Luring Westerners with Low-Cost Surgeries' Dallas Morning News, November 16, 2005

[37] http://www.ehirc.com/images/ehirc_package.pdf

[38] Herzilnger, Market Driven Healthcare, page 281

[39] David Hogberg, 'Healthcare's Godmother' The American Spectator ' 5/22/2007

www.ingramcontent.com/pod-product-compliance
Lightning Source LLC
Chambersburg PA
CBHW060504290526
45791CB00001B/265